"WAR" IN LIFE INSURANCE CONTRACTS

"War" in Life Insurance Contracts:

Judicial Interpretation of Its Meaning 1945-1975

Dorothy Schaffter

An *Exposition-University Book*

EXPOSITION PRESS HICKSVILLE, NEW YORK

The author has received written permission from the copyright owners to quote materials from their publications as they appear in this volume, on condition that full acknowledgment be given to the author and to the publication.

In two cases owners specified the form of acknowledgment:

> Reprinted with permission from *Villanova Law Review*, Vol. 3, No. 1, pp. 107-109. © Copyright by Villanova University.
>
> Reprinted by permission of the Yale Law Journal Company and Fred B. Rothman and Company from *The Yale Law Journal*, Vol. 56, pp. 748-52.

FIRST EDITION

Library of Congress Catalog Card Number: 76-684

ISBN 0-682-48477-6

Printed in the United States of America

CONTENTS

INTRODUCTION

In the thirty-year period between 1943 and 1973 many cases involving the meaning of the word "war" in life insurance contracts were tried in different state and federal courts. It might appear that, given so many cases over such a long period of time, an authoritative definition would have evolved, but such is not the case. Attention is called to the related fact that these insurance cases were not the only ones in which such definition was sought with very limited success. Numerous cases were tried in military courts, under the code of military justice, involving members of the armed forces. In the state and federal courts even more cases appeared involving persons seeking exemption from military service either before or after induction.

As a result, judicial determinations of the definition of "war" are so numerous and so widely different that confusion has been produced. With the conclusion of the Vietnamese conflict it is to be hoped that the situation will permit an effort to reconcile these definitions, resulting in one generally accepted in the different federal, state and military courts in their respective jurisdictions.

The present study deals with only one part of this problem —that is, the definition of "war," as the term is used in life insurance contracts, in cases decided since World War II.

Briefly, the five parts of the study deal respectively with cases arising from three major conflicts (World War II, the Korean conflict, and the conflict in Southeast Asia), in the fourth section there are relevant selections from articles in professional insurance journals, bar association journals and law reviews, and the fifth section contains certain recommendations for reform. The first group of cases includes those arising from events on

Pearl Harbor day, December 7, 1941, preceding congressional action on the following day, and those arising from cessation of hostilities following World War II but preceding formal declaration of the end of the war. The period of *declared* war between formal declaration and formal termination is not considered because the cases arising during that period did not hinge on a definition of war. Since there were no declarations of war preceding the conflicts in Korea and Southeast Asia, many cases did require definition of "war" as the term was used in life insurance contracts held by members of the armed forces who were killed during those conflicts.

Throughout the thirty years between 1943 and 1973 decisions of state and federal courts alternated between two theories in their definitions of "war." One line of decisions, in its effect favoring the insured, was based on a legalistic interpretation which required that Congress must formally declare a "war." The other line, favoring the insurer, defined "war" realistically by taking into consideration the undisputed fact that there was common knowledge of the existence of war, and that many executive and legislative actions (short of formal declaration) also furnished recognition of such existence.

The facts in the cases under consideration were essentially the same. Many young men of military age had taken life insurance policies containing the usual provisions for payment to a beneficiary in case of death. These provisions were not contested by the insurance companies. The problems arose from the inclusion in the policies of "war exclusion" clauses and provision for double indemnity in cases of accidental death. These provisions resulted in a very large number of claims by beneficiaries. Many different legal points were raised, among them the definition of the word "war"—the only point under consideration in the present study. Several articles contain discussion of the entire situation[1] if readers wish to go into it.

The following three sections in this introductory chapter are short essays, each summarizing an important aspect of the general subject. (1) Since the numerous cases all involved insurance contracts, the principles established in interpreting such contracts affected decisions specifically involving definition of the term "war." (2) The respective powers of the Congress and the President in initiating war were interpreted by the courts, and general principles were stated with respect to the judicial branch's obligation to take notice of such actions. (3) A brief section deals with U.S. Supreme Court action in the three instances in which it was called upon to act.

(1) General Principles of Insurance Contract Law

All the cases involving the definition of war as the term is used in life insurance contracts were decided under certain well-established principles of insurance-contract law, and many opinions of judges and professional journal articles contain discussion of these principles at length. Without attempting comprehensive treatment of them, it is possible to state them briefly as an aid to understanding of basic principles which affected the determination of the meaning of the term "war":

(1) An insurance policy is a simple contract, the provisions of which should be construed as any other type of contract.

(2) The right of an insured to recover under a life policy should not be left to depend upon determination of a question not governable by definite test either legal or factual, but its terms and conditions should be interpreted according to some definite and uniform standard.

(3) Words and phrases in an insurance contract are used and intended to be used in their legal sense.

(4) A contract phrase, if susceptible of two interpretations, must be given that which accords with settled law.

(5) The words in an insurance policy will be given the meaning that common speech imports, unless it is obvious that they are intended to be used in a more technical connotation.

(6) If the language of an insurance policy is reasonably

opened to two constructions, that most favorable to the insured will be adopted.

(7) Limitations to and exclusions from the coverage of a policy must be clearly expressed, and in case of doubt are construed unfavorably to the insurer who drafted the policy.

(8) A court may not and should not create an imaginary ambiguity in order to construe a contract against the insurer.

(9) Construction of an unambiguous contract is a question of law for the court and the cardinal rule for construction is to ascertain the intention of the parties.

(10) In all private matters, unaffected by the public interest, parties are free to contract with reference to war and to give it such definition, connotation and meaning as does not infringe upon public policy.

(11) In construing an insurance policy, the court's function and duty is to ascertain and effectuate the lawful intention of the parties, and in so doing the court should place itself in the position of the parties when the contract was made and should consider the purposes, subject matter, and circumstances under which their minds met.

One does not have to read this list of principles beyond the fifth in order to discover that the "well-established principles" of insurance contract law, most unfortunately, contain *contradictory* principles. For example, principles 3 and 5 and 11 should be compared. Three standards of interpretation are stated—words and phrases in policies are to be interpreted (3) in their legal or technical sense, or (5) with the meaning which common speech and general understanding import, or (11) with the meaning and intention of the parties to the contract. Understandably, this situation has led to the disagreements between the many courts which have been compelled to define the term "war," resulting in two lines of decisions. The insured benefits if the legal definition is accepted—the insurer benefits if the common meaning definition is accepted—and one party *or* the other may benefit depending upon the court's ability to determine the intent of the parties.

(2) *The Three Branches of Government and the Definition of War*

A formal declaration of war by Congress acting under its constitutional authority undoubtedly results in "war," and if all the conflicts in which the United States has participated had followed such declaration there would be no questions about the meaning of the term in life insurance contracts. There are, however, four periods in recent history during which armed conflict occurred (December 7, 1941 preceding formal declaration of war on the following day, the period after cessation of hostilities and preceding formal peace declaration following World War II, the conflict in Korea, and the conflict in Southeast Asia) even though no formal congressional declaration of war had authorized it. Consequently, the use of the term "war" in life insurance contracts was placed in question, if attempts by beneficiaries to collect under the policies came before the courts.

The results of decisions in these cases are conflicting as is demonstrated by the following quotations from opinions:

(1) Courts will take judicial notice of beginning, existence and ending of all wars in which the United States has participated.

(2) The judicial branch of the government is bound by and must follow the action of the political branches of the government, in determining whether the country is at war.

(3) In determining judicial questions concerning commencement or termination of a state of war, courts are generally required to refer to some public act of the political department of the government.

(4) The United States becomes "engaged in war" whenever Congress makes a declaration of war or the congressional

or executive authority of the government recognizes that a state of war exists, and such status continues until the legislative or executive authority, or both, recognize and declare that the United States is no longer engaged.

(5) Until there has been a declaration by the proper department of government that war exists, the courts cannot take judicial notice of the existence of war by their government.

(6) [Same as above, except that] it must be an act or recognition by the department of government clothed with the war-making power.

(7) Numerous examples of congressional action recognize the fact of war in Korea, without formal declaration.

(8) The existence of a state of war as determined by political departments of government is binding upon courts only in matters of public concern, while as to private contracts the governing principle is the real intent of the parties.

In many of the above statements there is reference to the "legislative and executive departments," the latter presumably meaning the President, but the different opinions in these cases contain very few direct references to his power as Commander in Chief. In view of the great interest in the early 1970s in this source of his authority, it is remarkable that it attracted so little attention in the life insurance contract cases. These cases have, however, contained some statements, quoted below:

(1) President Franklin D. Roosevelt: message of December 8, 1941. I ask that Congress declare that, since the unprovoked and dastardly attack by Japan on Sunday, December 7, a state of war has existed between the United States and the Japanese Empire.

(2) Public Law 328, 77th Congress, Chap. 561, 1st Sess.; 50 U.S.C.A. (1943) p. 68.

That the state of war between the United States and the Imperial Government of Japan which has thus been thrust upon the United States is hereby formally declared; and the President is hereby authorized and directed to employ the entire naval and military forces. . . . to carry on war against the Imperial Government of Japan; . . .

(3) The President's message of December 8, 1941 was an official act in conformity with his duty as Commander in Chief; it did not and could not amount to a legal determination of or a declaration of the existence of a state of war.

(4) U.S. armed forces, under authority of the Commander in Chief, immediately after commencement of the attack on December 7, 1941, entered the combat and succeeded in repelling the invasion. This was war. The President as Commander in Chief could not wait for Congress to declare war officially.

(5) We are not here concerned with the constitutional authority of the President to dispatch troops to Korea to repel armed aggression against the Republic of Korea, generally conceded to be in pursuance of article 39 of the United Nations Charter. Our concern is whether the nation has thereby been committed to an undeclared war of which we must take judicial notice. Without declaration by Congress this is not a war.

(6) Danger to the life of its assured, and so liability on the part of the company, would be no less because the chief executive, using his power and authority as Commander in Chief of the armed forces of the United States, committed us to a conflict with other nations without the constitutional sanction of a formal declaration by the Congress. . . It made no difference to either party to the contract whether the Congress acted; the executive committed us to a real and bitter war. Nor was this in any sense unusual. . . In fact, it has long been recognized that the executive may, in many ways, embroil his country in war, so that the legislature has no opportunity to prevent it and no choice but to accept it as an accomplished fact.

Without oversimplifying a complex situation, it seems to offer several options. "War" as the term has been defined in case law may result from (1) action by the President alone under his constitutional authority as Commander in Chief; (2) such action, followed by a retroactive declaration of war by Congress under its constitutional authority; (3) a declaration of war by Congress as the only legal authority; (4) actions by Congress confirming its recognition of the existence of war, although there has been no formal declaration; (5) undefined acts of the "political branches of government"; and (6) "some public act" of these branches. Points (1) and (2) were involved in the cases arising out of events on Pearl Harbor day, December 7, 1941, preceding Congress's declaration of war on the following day, but they did not arise in cases involving the Korean and Southeast Asian conflicts. In the latter cases points (4), (5) and (6) were involved. The general rule was accepted by the courts—that they will take judicial notice of the beginning, existence and end of all wars in which the United States has participated. That left the major question—the definition of "war."

(3) Decisions by the U.S. Supreme Court

The Supreme Court of the United States has had three opportunities to consider cases on appeal:

New York Life Ins. Co. v. Bennion (1946)
Beley v. Pennsylvania Mut. Life Ins. Co. *and*
  Harding v. Pennsylvania Mut. Life Ins. Co. (1953)
Western Reserve Life Ins. Co. v. Meadows (1954)

Bennion was on appeal from the Circuit Court of Appeals, 10th District; *Beley* and *Harding* from the Supreme Court of Pennsylvania, and *Meadows* from the Supreme Court of Texas. There were no dissents in the U.S. Supreme Court decisions, and no opinions were filed. In each case the appeal was based on a writ of certiorari, and the Supreme Court, in each case, denied the appeal.

It might be expected that these actions of the Supreme Court would have caused considerable comment, but this was not the case. The results of the three decisions may, from one point of view, be considered to be consistent—the Supreme Court signaled that, for reasons of its own, it would uphold the decisions of State supreme courts and inferior federal courts even if they were conflicting. But the results of the Court's decisions were not consistent insofar as their effects on the definition of war—*Beley* and *Harding* upheld the legalistic definition of the term, and *Bennion* and *Meadows* upheld the "common understanding" definition.

In a few cases law-review authors have expressed their opinions on the situation:

Samuel J. Goldstein, the attorney for the plaintiff in *Beley* before the Pennsylvania Supreme Court, wrote:[2]

> The insurance carrier in the *Beley* case on June 22, 1953, filed a petition for writ of certiorari in the United States Supreme Court. However, it does not appear that any federal question is involved which would enable the Supreme Court to take jurisdiction, especially since no federal or constitutional question was raised during the proceedings or arguments. The Supreme Court has not yet acted upon the petition and it would appear to be a foregone conclusion that the writ of certiorari will be denied.

J. W. Wheeler, the attorney for the insurance company in *Meadows*, agreed with Goldstein's judgment:[3]

> . . . but it does not appear from examination of the briefs [in *Beley*] that a federal question is clearly, if at all, presented, and it is doubtful if the Supreme Court will take jurisdiction on this application. [Attention was called to Goldstein's article in which he wrote] that it would appear to be a foregone conclusion that the writ of certiorari would be denied. If the Supreme Court does deny the writ of certiorari in the *Beley* case, the fact that no federal or constitutional question was presented should be sufficient to rebut any argument that the Supreme Court of the United States, by denial of the writ, has approved the decision of the Supreme Court of Pennsylvania in the *Beley* case.

Goldstein's and Wheeler's predictions as to the action of the Supreme Court proved to be correct. Since no appeals have been taken from the decisions of state supreme courts and federal lower courts since Meadows in 1954, it would appear that plaintiffs and defendants alike have accepted as a fact the Supreme Court's unwillingness to hear this type of case on appeal.

Conclusion

The purpose of the present study is to make available a very considerable amount of primary information on a subject of immediate concern. There are, to be sure, several excellent treatments in the professional journals, but secondary sources never take the place, for the serious student of a subject, of access to the primary materials. Seeking such access—as the author can testify—is a very time-consuming process and it can be conducted only in first-class law and insurance company libraries, such as those found in Washington.

The collected materials in the study do not support a single, established definition of the term "war" as it is used in life insurance contracts. The reader is left with a choice between two definitions:

> The word "war" when used in a private contract or document should not be construed on a public or political basis, in a legalistic or technical sense, but should be given its ordinary, usual and realistic meaning, viz., actual hostilities between the armed forces of two or more nations or states de facto or de jure (*Stanbery v. Aetna Life Ins. Co.*, 98 A.2d 134 (1953), at 138).

> The existence or nonexistence of a state of war is a political, not a judicial, question and it is only when a formal declaration of war has been made by Congress that judicial cognizance may be taken thereof and once so declared by the political department, it becomes binding upon the parties, otherwise not. (*Pyramid Life Insurance Company v. John William Masch*, 299 P. 2d 117 (1956) at 117).

Notes

1. [No author] Date of war inception as determinant of liability in life insurance contracts. *Yale Law Journal*, v. 56, April 1947, pp. 746-752.

   Smith, Calvin E. The meaning and effect of military service

and war exception clauses in life insurance policies. *Duke Bar Journal,* v. 3, Fall 1952, pp. 11-20.

Goldstein, Samuel J. The war clause in life insurance contracts. *Insurance Law Journal,* v. 1953, July 1953, pp. 458-478.

Crain, James M. War exclusion clauses and undeclared wars. *Tennessee Law Review,* v. 39, Winter 1972, pp. 328-339.

2. The war clause in life insurance contracts. *Insurance Law Journal,* v. 1953, July 1953, pp. 458-478, at p. 478.
3. The war clause. *Insurance Law Journal,* v. 370, November 1953, pp. 727-737, at p. 732.

1

WORLD WAR II

Introduction

Between 1943 and 1949 two lines of decisions in cases involving life insurance clearly established two different judicial doctrines. In the most simple terms, one series contained decisions in which courts held that there could be no war without declaration by the Congress—often referred to as a "legalistic" position. In contrast, several courts took a more "practical" or "realistic" position, holding that the presence of actual hostilities constituted war for the purposes of deciding the cases involved.

These cases arose either as a result of events on December 7, 1941—the day before Congress formally declared war on Japan—or events after the cessation of hostilities in World War II but preceding the signing of peace treaties. Between these two periods there existed a "declared" war, and cases arising from events in these years are not relevant to the present considerations.

Chronologically, four cases decided in 1943-1945 held that war did not exist on December 7, 1941 when the Pearl Harbor attack occurred. It existed only when Congress declared war on December 8. In 1946 the first decision reversing the earlier line of decisions was rendered. In 1947 one case followed the earlier line but this decision was reversed in 1948. In the several cases in 1948 and 1949 the definition of war was established involving events after the cessation of hostilities but preceding the signing of peace treaties. In every case the courts decided that "war" was terminated when hostilities ceased.

1. *Declaration of War by Congress as the Definition of War*

West v. Palmetto State Life Ins. Co.,[1] tried before the Supreme Court of South Carolina, established the principles followed, in general, by the courts which rendered decisions in later cases in this category. As a summary, the headnotes in *West v. Palmetto* are quoted below:

> 1. *War*
> "War" is a contest by force between two or more nations, carried on for any purpose or armed conflict of sovereign powers or declared and open hostilities, or the state of nations among whom there is an interruption of pacific relations, and a general contention by force authorized by the sovereign.
>
> 2. *War*
> Under federal constitutional provision that Congress shall have the power to declare war, an act of Congress is necessary to the commencement of a foreign war and is in itself a "declaration" and fixes the date of the war. U.S.C.A. Const. art. 1, § 8.
>
> 3. *Constitutional law*
> The courts are bound by a declaration by the proper department of government that a war exists. U.S.C.A. Const. art. 1, § 8.
>
> 4. *Evidence*
> Until there has been a declaration by the proper department of government that a war exists, the courts cannot take judicial notice of the existence of a war by their government. U.S.C.A. Const. art. 1, § 8.
>
> 5. *War*
> Under constitutional provision that Congress shall have the power to declare war, a declaration by the United States Congress of war upon Japan was the only legal way in which the United States could be placed in a state of war with Japan. U.S.C.A. Const. art. 1, § 8.
>
> 6. *Insurance*
> Death of insured seaman in the United States Navy at Pearl Harbor on December 7, 1941, resulting from the bombing attack by the Japanese government did not occur in time of "war" within provisions of life policies limiting insurer's liability when insured is engaged in military or naval service in time of war in view that actual declaration of war was not made by Congress until the following day. Joint Resolution December 8, 1941, 50 U.S.C.A. Appendix, note preceding section 1; U.S.C.A. Const. art. 1, § 8.

The South Carolina court had little in the way of precedent

upon which to depend. The opinion quoted dictionary definitions and statements from *Corpus Juris* as follows:

> The definition of war in Corpus Juris, 67 C.J. 336, is as follows: "War in the legal sense is the state of nations among whom there is an interruption of all pacific relations and a general contestation of arms by authority of the several sovereigns; it is not a mere contest of force, but must be an armed struggle carried on between two political bodies each of which exercises de facto authority over persons within a determinate territory, and its existence is determined by the authorized political department of the government. So, lawful war can never exist without the actual concurrence of the war-making power, but may exist prior to any contest of the armed forces. The courts are bound by a declaration or determination by the proper department of government that a war exists, while until there has been such a declaration or determination the courts cannot take judicial notice of the existence of a war by their government."
>
> Very pointed is the following from the same Volume, Page 338: "A court cannot, however, take judicial notice of a war by its government until there has been some act or declaration creating or recognizing the existence of war by the department of the government clothed with the war-making power."

The opinion in *Palmetto* continued:

> It is seen from the foregoing authorities that the declaration by Congress of war on Japan on December 8th was the only legal way in which this country could be placed in a state of war with that aggressor nation. The Constitution so provides, Art. 1, Sec. 8, supra. That the policy contracts were entered into by the parties in contemplation of that clear law, and subject to it, cannot be denied; and they are bound by it.
>
> Appellant relies strongly upon two decisions from other jurisdictions (Vanderbilt v. Travelers' Ins. Co., 112 Misc. 248, 184 N.Y.S. 54, and Stankus v. New York L. Ins. Co. 1942, 312 Mass. 366, 44 N.E.2d 687) which upon consideration we do not think are contrary in reason or conclusion to our view of the instant case. They involved respectively, a death upon the S.S. Lusitania, sunk by German submarine long prior to the commencement of our war in 1917-18 against the Central Powers, and a death upon the destroyer Reuben James, lost on patrol in the Atlantic months before the commencement of our present war with

Germany. But the policy provisions in question in those cases were quite different from those that are now under consideration. In one the policy excluded liability "if the insured's death resulted from war or any act incident thereto." And the other policy denied coverage for "death resulting, directly or indirectly, wholly or partly, from war." The policies in the present appeal contained restrictive provisions effective when the insured was "engaged in military or naval service in time of war," as pointed out above, very clearly meaning the engagement of the insured in such service of his country "in time of war."

[6] And this case was fought out in the court below upon the question, stated hereinabove, whether our present war with Japan had begun on December 7, 1941, when the insured died as the result of Japanese attack on that day, and the controversy has not concerned itself with whether the insured died as the result, direct or indirect, of just any war, as was the question in the cited cases. Appellant recognized this narrow view of the issue presented in the opening paragraph of its printed brief and said: "The only real question for the consideration of the Court is whether on December 7, 1941, the United States of America, in the armed forces of which young West was then serving, was at war ***." We think it clear that the stated question should be, and it is, answered in the negative.

We are impressed with respondent's argument that it would be as logical to contend that the attack by the Emperor's fliers upon the U.S.S. Panay in the Yangtze river several years before was the beginning of the present war, as to so contend with respect to the sneak surprise attack on Pearl Harbor. The incidents do appear to have differed only in magnitude and location, and the declaration of war more promptly followed the latter. Japan's pretensive claim of mistake of identity in the case of the Panay has been discredited; it is believed that it was intended to test the will of this nation to resist aggression.

The exceptions are overruled and the judgments affirmed.

It will be noted that there is no reference in this opinion to the power of the President as Commander-in-Chief in relation to the existence of war, as evidenced by his message to Congress on December 8, 1941.

The second case in this series, *Rosenau v. Idaho Mut. Ben. Ass'n.*,[2] followed *Palmetto* very closely. The opinion contained a statement of some importance in the present connection:

While the President's message of December 8th containing his summation of the many unprovoked, premeditated and dastardly attacks of the previous day, by the military and naval forces of the Imperial Japanese government, on our armed forces and territory, and at a time when we were at peace with that government, was an official act in conformity with his duty as Commander-in-Chief of the army and navy, and paved the way for the declaration of war on our part, which immediately followed, it in itself did not and could not amount to a legal determination of or a declaration of the existence of a state of war on the part of the American people, since the power to declare war is fixed solely in the Congress, by art. 1, sec. 8, of the Federal Constitution, which provides that the Congress has power to declare war.

The opinion continued with citation to *Palmetto,* and definitions of war and case citations contained in the *Palmetto* opinion. It further cited the *Prize Cases (The Army Warwick),*[3] which arose out of the Civil War, and *Hamilton v. McClaughry,*[4] which arose out of the Boxer Rebellion, with this conclusion:

In these cases the political and executive department of our government had authorized the warlike acts, out of which the litigation arose, while in the instant case no act or recognition had taken place by any department of our government with regard to the existence of war, or warlike activities, at the time of the death of the insured. (In fact, at that very time the two countries were engaged in peaceful negotiations, Japan's Kuruso, special ambassador of so-called "good will" being even then present in Washington ostensibly trying to obtain a peaceful settlement of the controversies between the two governments.) This, not having been done, this court, under the facts in this case, can not hold that this nation was at war on December 7, 1941, at the time of the death of the insured, or at any time prior to the declaration by the Congress on December 8, 1941.

The rule by which we are bound here is well stated in *Bishop* v. *Jones,* 28 Tex. 294 (319), as follows: " 'War' in its legal sense, has been aptly defined to be "the state of nations among whom there is an interruption of all pacific relations and a general contestation of arms authorized by the sovereign.' It is true it may and has frequently in latter times been commenced and carried on without either a notice or declaration, but still there can be no war by its government of which the court can take judicial knowledge until there has been some act or declaration creating or recognizing its existence by that department of the government clothed with the war-making power."

The Chief Justice of the Supreme Court of Idaho rendered the opinion in *Rosenau.* Two justices concurred and two dissented. Quotation from the dissenting opinion follows:

It will be observed, from the message of the President, that, so far as the Commander in Chief of the Army and Navy of the United States was concerned, *hostilities existed;* and that such hostilities commenced when the Japanese armed forces "attacked by naval and air forces"—"the United States of America." It will also be observed that the President asked the Congress to "declare that, *since* the unprovoked and dastardly attack. . . . on Sunday, December 7, *a state of war has existed.*" We are therefore confronted with the record made by the President, as Commander in Chief of the Army and Navy, that "a state of war has existed . . . since . . . Sunday, December 7th"; and that, "as Commander in Chief of the Army and Navy", he had "directed that all measures be taken for our defense."

Immediately following the message of the President, the following resolution passed both the House and Senate:

"Whereas the Imperial Government of Japan has committed unprovoked acts of war against the Government and the people of the United States of America: Therefore be it

"*Resolved by the Senate and House of Representatives of the United States of America in Congress assembled,* That the state of war between the United States and the Imperial Government of Japan *which has thus been thrust upon the United States* is hereby *formally declared;* and the President is hereby authorized and directed to employ the entire naval and military forces of the United States and the resources of the Government to carry on war against the Imperial Government of Japan; and, to bring the conflict to a successful termination, all of the resources of the country are hereby pledged by the Congress of the United States." (Italics inserted. Public Law 328—77th Congress—chap. 561 1st Sess.; 50 U.S.C.A., Appendix (1943), p. 68.)

Congress accordingly declared that "the state of war between the United States and the Imperial Government of Japan . . . has thus been thrust upon the United States" and "is hereby formally declared." In other words, the resolution by Congress was an acknowledgement and recognition of both the state and condition of war, having its inception in the "unprovoked acts of war against the Government and the people of the United States", [Pub. Law 328, 77th Cong. S.J.Res. 116] committed on the previous day, (December 7th) at Pearl Harbor. It seems clear that the Congress did not consider or intend that the resolution was the *commencement* of the war; it was rather an acknowledgement of the existence of war which commenced the day before. It was official recognition of a status already existent.

Reference to the Congressional Record discloses that most of the members of the House of Representatives, who spoke officially for adoption of the resolution, understood that war already existed. "We are at war", said different members. (P. 9529, vol. 87, part 9, Cong. Record.) It is clear from the record, that all the members of Congress thought and understood that they were declaring the existence of an attack and acts of war already committed by the armed forces of the Japanese government; and that they did not consider they were initiating or starting the war on behalf of the United States by the passage of the resolution acknowledging the existence of a state of war.

In the face of these facts and records, we are confronted with the question: What is war? There may be room for doubt and argument as to whether a fight (war) is on as soon as the first blow is struck; but there is little room for doubt that a *fight* (war) is on when the adversary returns blow for blow and the contest of strength and endurance begins.

After describing the events at Pearl Harbor on December 7, 1941 the dissenting opinion continued:

According to the official report, the United States armed forces, under the authority of the Commander in Chief of Army and Navy, immediately after the commencement of the attack, entered the combat and succeeded in repelling the invasion. This it seems to me, was "war." The President as Commander of Chief of the Army and Navy could not wait for Congress to officially declare war. He accordingly ordered into action all available naval, air and military forces to repel the attempted invasion.

I think the average citizen, who might apply for and procure a life insurance policy, containing the war clause here in question, would undoubtedly think and believe that such a national military status was war; and he would not believe himself insured against such a casualty.

Respondents place their chief reliance on *West v. Palmetto State Life Insurance Co.*, 202 S.C. 422, 25 S.E. (2d) 475, 145 A.L.R. 1461. Notwithstanding the high esteem which I entertain for the South Carolina court, I am unable to follow or adopt its course of reasoning or conclusion in that case.

Under the contention made by respondents, an insurance policy non-liability war clause can never be available as a defense unless Congress has, previously to the death of the insured, formally declared war—no matter what the President as Commander in Chief may have done in defense of the country against invasion, although evidenced by executive statement and the records of the war department. If that contention were true and were followed by the courts, insurance companies would be issuing policies containing the war clause in question and always be liable on the death of the insured in every undeclared war, no matter how long prosecuted or what the result might be.

Our political history demonstrates that most wars have been commenced and prosecuted without any formal declaration of war; and that war dates from its *inception* rather than from the time on which some formal declaration to that effect is made. In the Stankus case above cited, the Massachusetts court had the following to say on this point: [312 Mass. 368, 44 N.E. (2d) at 688]:

"The plaintiff contends that the policy exempts only a death that resulted from a war in which the United States was a participant, and that as this government was not engaged in any war on October 30, 1941, the death of the insured could not have resulted from a war as that term was employed in the policy. The government of the United States had not at that time declared war upon any nation (see 55 U.S. Sts. at Large, cc. 561, 564, 565, passed December 8, 1941, and December 11, 1941), declaring war upon Japan, Germany and Italy, and no nation had then declared war against us. But the *existence of a war is not dependent upon a formal declaration of war.* Wars are being waged today that began without any declaration of war. *The attack by the Japanese on Pearl Harbor on December 7, 1941, is the latest illustration.* This is not a modern method, for it has been said that, from out of one hundred eighteen wars that occurred between 1700 and 1872, in hardly ten did formal declarations precede the commencement of hostilities." (Italics inserted.)

It is my conclusion, that the judgment in this case should be reversed.

A third case was decided by the District Court, W.D., Louisiana, Monroe Division, in 1944—*Savage v. Sun Life Assur. Co. of Canada.*[5] It followed *Palmetto* and *Rosenau* but attention is called to a very slight change in wording, both in headnote 2 and in the text of the opinion (p. 621):

> 2. *War*
> "War" does not exist merely because of an armed attack by the military forces of another nation until it is a condition recognized or accepted by political authority of government which is attacked, *either through an actual declaration of war or other acts demonstrating such position.* [Italics added.]

These last five words broaden the definition in the two preceding cases, which clearly stated that the *only* legal method of establishing the existence of war was a formal declaration by Congress under its constitutional power. The text of the opinion does not expand on the brief statement in headnote 2.

A fourth decision by an Hawaiian trial court in August, 1944 was reversed by the Hawaiian circuit court the following year. The latter case was *Gladys Ching Pang v. Sun Life Assurance Company of Canada.*[6] The trial court maintained that the United States was at war on December 7, 1941. The Circuit Court First Circuit in reversing this decision cited *Palmetto, Rosenau* and *Savage* as precedents.

Judicial notice was taken of the President's message of December 8, a public document, from which this sentence was quoted:

> I ask that the Congress declare that, since the unprovoked and dastardly attack by Japan on Sunday, December 7, a state of war has existed between the United States and the Japanese Empire.

Quoting the opinion:

It was probably within the power of Congress to comply with the request of the President to declare the preexistence of a state of war. The Act declaring war with Spain, passed and approved by the President on April 25, 1898, declared that war be and the same is hereby declared to exist, and that war has existed since April 21, 1898, including said day, between the United States of America and the Kingdom of Spain. (30 Stats. 364). We must therefore construe the joint resolution which the Congress passed in response to the President's message to determine whether or not the Congress did what the President asked it to do.

Counsel argues that Congress did exactly what the President asked it to do. The discussion of the joint resolution of 1917 declaring war on Germany would seem to refute this argument.

We shall now notice the cases relied upon by the defendant.

[At pp. 218-221, these cases were reviewed.]

All of the cases upon which the defendant bases its claim that within the meaning of the exclusion clause of the policy we were at war with Japan from the moment of the attack on December 7, 1941, recognize that an armed conflict, to be commonly regarded as war, must be between two nations under authority of their respective governments. See the *Stankus* case, *supra,*[7] strongly relied upon by the defendant to establish its claim that the death of insured resulted from war, where it is said, "A conflict between the armed forces of two nations under authority of their respective governments would be commonly regarded as war."

Applying the foregoing rule of construction to the clause excluding double indemnity, if the death of the insured resulted from war or any act incident thereto, we find it impossible, in the light of said rule and the authorities to which we have referred, to agree with the defendant's contention that the death of the insured resulted from war within the meaning of the exclusion clause of the policy.

The exception to the decision and the judgment is therefore sustained.

2. *Definition of War Without Declaration by Congress*

The decision in the case of *New York Life Ins. Co. v. Bennion*[8] in 1946 was based on the principle which had been supported by the dissenting minority of the court in the *Rosenau* case. Two of the Circuit Judges in *Bennion* agreed that the attack on Pearl Harbor on December 7, 1941 constituted war for the purposes of construing and interpreting life policies, and one judge wrote an opinion in dissent.

Because *Bennion* was the first in a series of cases to accept a definition of war without a formal declaration by Congress, and because the decision was not reversed by the United States Supreme Court, the majority opinion is quoted rather extensively below:

> [1] No one denies the grim reality that the attack beginning December 7, 1941, at about 7:30 A.M. Honolulu time, marked the commencement of an armed conflict between two sovereign nations which ended only when the Japanese surrendered nearly four years later. Furthermore, it seems to be agreed that the existence or non-existence of a state of war is a political question, to be determined by the political department of our Government. The basic difference lies in the contention on the one hand that a formal declaration by the Congress, which alone has the constitutional power to declare and make war, is an essential prerequisite to judicial cognizance of its existence; and the contention on the other hand that the existence of a war is not dependent upon its formal declaration, but rather is determinable from an appraisal of actualities; that the formal declaration by Congress on the day after the attack was merely a formal recognition of that which was already actually in existence. Both contentions find very respectable support in the adjudicated cases. Since the contract was made in Virginia, its construction and effect are of course governed by Virginia law. But the Virginia courts have not spoken, and we therefore have the duty to determine what we conceive will be the law of Virginia when its courts do speak on the subject.
>
> All of the cases which support the appellee involve the death of an insured resulting from the Pearl Harbor attack under contracts of insurance, containing either identical or similar words of exclusion as those under consideration here. They are bottomed on the concept that courts may not take judicial notice of the existence of a war until it is formally and officially declared by the Congress of the United States; that the parties contracted in contemplation of this rule of law and are bound by it. A valid distinction is drawn between an act of war

and a state of war, and the attack of December 7th is characterized as an act of war, which did, but not necessarily, eventuate in a state of war. The Panay Incident on the Yangtze River in China is suggested as a comparable act of war which did not eventuate in a state of war. Then too, it is said, in accordance with the universal rule, that if the words used to express the intention of the parties in the contract are ambiguous or susceptible of two meanings, one of which will permit recovery and the other will not, it should be given a construction most favorable to the insured.

[*Palmetto, Rosenau, Savage,* and *Pang* were cited, and the present case was compared with cases based on events in World War I and the Civil War.]

[2] When one sovereign nation attacks another with premeditated and deliberate intent to wage war against it, and that nation resists the attacks with all the force at its command, we have war in the grim sense of reality. It is war in the only sense that men know and understand it. Mankind goes no further in his definitive search—he does not stand on ceremony or wait for technical niceties. To say that courts must shut their eyes to realities and wait for formalities, is to cut off the power to reason with concrete facts. We cannot believe that the courts are deprived of the power to deal with this vital question in a practical and realistic sense.

[3] Let us suppose that Congress was not in session on December 7th when the Japanese attacked, and could not convene for thirty days, therefore could not and did not formally declare or recognize a state of war until January 8, 1942. Meanwhile, the President, acting in his capacity as Commander and Chief of the armed forces, took all available measures, not only to repel the invasion, but waged, as we did, an offensive war at Midway and throughout the Pacific. And let us suppose that the insured here had been killed on January 7, 1942, in one of the many sea battles which raged over the Pacific immediately after the Pearl Harbor attack. In these circumstances, it cannot be denied that the acts and conduct of the President, acting in furtherance of his constitutional authority and duty, would constitute a political determination of a state of war of which the courts would take judicial notice. We can discern no demonstrable difference in the supposition and the actual facts, and we therefore conclude that the formal declaration by the Congress on December 8th was not an essential prerequisite to a political determination of the existence of a state of war commencing with the attack on Pearl Harbor.

[4] But the actual existence of a state of war and the political determination of its commencement with the attack on December 7th is immaterial to this lawsuit if the word war, as used in the contract, was intended by the parties to mean a state of war which commenced only with a formal declaration by Congress on December 8th. In construing and interpreting the contract between the parties, it is our function and duty to ascertain and effectuate their lawful intention. In so doing, we should place ourselves in the position of the parties when the contract was made, consider the purposes, the subject matter, and the circumstances under which their minds met. New York Casualty Co. v. Sinclair Refining Co., 10 Cir., 108 F.2d 65; Cocke v. Vacuum Oil Co., 5 Cir., 63 F.2d 406; Western Commercial Travelers' Ass'n v. Smith, 8 Cir., 85 F. 401, 40 L. R.A. 653; Restatement of Contracts, Sec. 226 & 236.

[5] The subject matter of the contract was a risk assumed on the life of the insured by the Company, for a stipulated premium, and the use of the word war was obviously intended to denote a restriction or limitation upon the risk assumed. It is plain, therefore, that the definition given to the word war bears a direct relationship to the risk assumed, which is the subject matter of the contract. Viewed in this light, it is also plain that when the parties used the word war, they had in mind the hazard to human life incident thereto. Virginia courts adhere to the general rule that, as in other contracts, words used in insurance contracts to express the intent of the parties are to be construed in their plain, ordinary and popular sense, unless it is evident from the general scope and purpose of the contract that the words were intended to have some other special meaning. United States Mutual Accident Ass'n. v. Newman, 84 Va. 52, 3 S.E. 805; Darden v. North American Ben. Ass'n, 170 Va. 479, 197 S.E. 413; Cooley Briefs on Ins., Vol. 2, p. 1004; Restatement of Contracts, Sec. 235; 29 Amer. Juris., Sec. 159, p. 175. Furthermore, the language used in the contract to express the intention of the parties is that of the Company, and it is only consistent with reason and justice that if a critical word or phrase in the policy is susceptible of more than one meaning, one of which permits recovery and the other does not, it should be given the construction most favorable to the insured. United States Mutual Accident Ass'n v. Newman, supra; Marandino v. Lawyers' Title Ins. Corp., 156 Va. 696, 159 S.E. 181; Strochmann v. Mutual Life Ins. Co. of New York, 300 U.S. 435, 57 S. Ct. 607, 81 L.Ed. 732; Bergholm v. Peoria Life Ins. Co., 284 U.S. 489, 52 S. Ct. 230, 76 L.Ed. 416.

[6] But we can find nothing in the subject matter, the context, or the purpose of this contract to indicate that the parties intended to use the word war in the technical sense of a formally declared war. The parties did not specify any particular type or kind of war, rather they used the all inclusive term, and we think it only fair to assume that they had in mind any type or kind of war in which the hazard of human life was involved. In short, we think the parties contracted with reference to a "shooting war". It follows therefore that the insured's death resulted from war or an act incident thereto within the meaning and purpose of the insurance policy.

• • •

The judgement is reversed.

HUXMAN, Circuit Judge (dissenting).

In my judgment, the decision of the lower court should be affirmed. In Gladys Ching Pang v. Sun Life Assur. Co. of Canada, decided at the October, 1945 term of the Supreme Court of the Territory of Hawaii, the court concluded that the attack on Pearl Harbor on December 7, 1941, did not constitute war so as to relieve an insurance company of liability under a similar exclusion clause. This is a well reasoned, exhaustive opinion, and I agree with its reasoning. The gist of this opinion is adopted for the purpose of this dissent. In addition to what is said in that case, I desire to make the following observations.

It is, of course, recognized without exception that where ambiguity exists in words or terms of an insurance contract, such ambiguity is most strongly construed against the insurance company and in favor of the insured. It is equally well recognized that a court may not and should not create an imaginary ambiguity in order to construe a contract against the company.

If the word "war" has but one meaning and is susceptible of exact definition so that the minds of reasonably intelligent men cannot differ as to its meaning, there is no occasion for the construction of the contract. It must, then, be given the one meaning which it has to men of such intelligence. But if, on the other hand, it has different meanings, or if what is war may have different meanings when considered in different settings, then there is ambiguity in the use of these terms in the contract, unless the sense in which they are used is clearly set out and defined.

"War" is a word of many meanings. It cannot be said that

it has but a single meaning. Neither does what constitutes war between nations mean the same things at all times. So there are acts of war, or acts of aggression, which, while they may lead to war, do not constitute war themselves. So, also, there is war in the legal sense, and in the material sense. Legal war exists when there is an interruption of all pacific relations between nations and an authorized contestation of armed forces by the constitutional authority of the nations, while material war is evidenced by the use of armed forces by the parties. It is said that war "is not a mere contest of force, but must be an armed struggle carried on between two political bodies each of which exercises de facto authority over persons within a determinate territory, and its existence is determined by the authorized political department of the government."[9]

In a legal sense, we are not and cannot be at war with another nation until Congress has declared war, either by a formal declaration of war or by an Act of Congress evidencing its consent to the waging of war, such as providing for the raising and equipping of armed forces, and authorizing the President to use them in combat with an aggressor nation. An act of aggression, whether large or small, by another nation, does not create a state of war until we accept the challenge in a way provided for under our Constitution. The President has power to resist acts of aggression, but he is powerless to declare war, go to war, or put us into war without the formal action of Congress expressed by some form of statutory enactment.

If we were at war with Japan during the attack on Pearl Harbor on December 7, we were likewise at war with Japan during the bombing of the Panay. The Panay incident is sought to be distinguished on the ground that it was unintentional on Japan's part, and the result of an accident. That was the explanation Japan gave, and we chose to accept it, because we did not at that time want to go to war. There is no doubt now that the Panay incident was deliberate, and I doubt if our government officials misunderstood it at the time. If the Pearl Harbor incident constituted war, then we were at war with Mexico when our fleet bombarded Vera Cruz, and we were at war with Mexico when our armed forces invaded Mexico in pursuit of Villa. Certainly the attack on Vera Cruz was just as deliberate as the attack on Pearl Harbor. There was no accident or misunderstanding in that attack. The gunfire from our warships was deliberately intentionally directed against the property of a sovereign nation, and killed Mexican citizens and destroyed Mexican property. Everyone knows that for a number of years, even before we went to war with Japan, the Japanese and Russian forces in Manchuria made numerous attacks on each other, some lasting for days. Yet both nations chose to ignore them and refused to go to war. During all this time they maintained their diplomatic relations and carried on their ordinary peacetime activities. It will be recalled that for a long time after we were at war with Japan, we urged Russia to sever diplomatic relations with Japan and go to war against her, but that Russia refused, and declared war and went to war against Japan only during the closing months of the war. Certainly, all of these acts of war which the Russian and Japanese forces committed against each other were deliberate and intentional. It cannot, however, be contended seriously that Russia and Japan were at war during the time of each of these incidents, extending over a number of years, but were then immediately at peace again when the incident was over, and were at war again when the next incident occurred, because during all of this time they continued their diplomatic relations and considered themselves to be at peace. These illustrations could be multiplied manyfold, but they suffice to show the distinction and difference between acts of aggression, which may or may not lead to war, and war itself. The only difference between the Pearl Harbor incident and the Panay and Vera Cruz incidents is one of degree. Those incidents did not lead to war. While the incident at Pearl Harbor did lead to war, it was legally possible to avoid war, and war did not come until it was declared.

Neither is the risk assumed for loss from acts of aggression between the armed forces of nations as great as loss from war. An act of aggression or an act of war may be a single incident or a limited number of incidents. Acts of aggression also cover a shorter period of time and are not waged with the same intensity as battles in war. As a result, an insurance company might well be willing to assume such risks, but not be willing to assume the enormous loss resulting from a legally declared war.

It seems to me that the word "war" and what constitutes war is susceptible of different meanings and incapable of exact definition. It follows that the sense in which these terms are used in the exclusion clause is ambiguous. While it may not be of legal significance, it is worthy of note on the question whether there is uncertainty in the mind of the company as to the ambiguity in the terms of the exclusion clause, that in another policy which we had occasion to consider in New York Life Ins. Co. v. Cooper, 10 Cir., 158 F. 2d 257, the language employed was entirely different. The language in that policy excluded loss from death resulting "*** from military or naval service in time of war; from a state of war, or insurrection." This language is certainly broader than the language in the policy in question here, and does not have the same meaning.

When ambiguity once exists, our duty under the well recognized rule of construction is clear. We do not gaze into a crystal ball to try to place ourselves in the position of the parties at the time of the execution of the contract in order to attune our minds to theirs, to try and think their thoughts as to how they would consider such a subsequent act as Pearl Harbor. The rule is clear that in such a case, we adopt the meaning most beneficial to the insured, and construe the contract most favorably to him. So construed, the ruling should be that the policy excludes loss from death resulting from war, meaning a legal war, but covers loss for death resulting from acts of aggression, whether they did or did not subsequently lead to war.

For the above reasons, I respectfully dissent.

3. *Termination of Hostilities as a Definition of War*

The difficult question of the date of the "end of World War II" was raised in *Stinson* (discussed below) and in several decisions rendered in 1948-1949. Did the German war end on the date of cessation of hostilities, or of the formal surrender, or on the signing of a peace treaty? Did the Japanese war end on cessation of hostilities, or of the formal surrender, or on the signing of a peace treaty? The German forces surrendered formally a considerable time before formal surrender in the Japanese war—did the "war" end insofar as the German portion of it was concerned, or did the "war" in both theatres continue until the Japanese portion was concluded? The answers to these questions were necessary in determination of the insurers' liability.

The opinions in the cases in 1948-1949 contained exhaustive discussion of these questions. The decisions followed *Stinson* and *Bennion* in holding that, from a practical standpoint, "war" with Japan and Germany ended with the cessation of hostilities in each case, for purposes of determining the liability of insurers. In no case was there a dissent.

The case of *Stinson v. New York Life Insurance Co.* was decided by the United States District Court of the District of Columbia in February, 1947, and in March, 1948 the Court of Appeals, District of Columbia reversed the earlier decision.[10]

The headnotes in the opinion by the District Court summarized the Court's decision:

> 1. *War*
> The United States becomes "engaged in war" whenever Congress makes a declaration of war or the congressional or executive authority of the government recognizes that a state of war exists, and such status continues until the legislative or executive authority, or both, recognize and declare that the United States is no longer engaged.
>
> 2. *Constitutional law*
> In determining whether country is still engaged in war notwithstanding hostilities have ceased, the judicial branch of the government is bound by and must follow the action of the political branches of the government.
>
> 3. *Insurance*
> The United States was a country "engaged in war" on October 2, 1945, when insured met his death in France while in military service of United States, within provision in life policy restricting payment to amount less than face value if insured's death occurred outside the home areas while he was in the military forces of any country "engaged in war", where there had been no proclamation by the executive that hostilities had ceased.

Quotation from relevant portions of the opinion follows:

> [1-3] The term [war] has a meaning so well recognized and of such long historical acceptation that it must be presumed to have been clearly understood not only by the insurer, but by the insured, at the time of his application for and acceptance of the policy here involved to have application to the situation here being considered. The United States becomes engaged in war whenever the Congress makes a declaration of war, or the congressional or executive authority of the Goverment recognizes that a state of war exists. The United States continues to be engaged in war until the legislative or executive authority, or both, recognize and declare that the United States is no longer

so engaged. The judicial branch of the Government must, in this matter, of necessity be bound by and follow the action of the political branches of the Government. The practical necessity and limitations upon the judicial process compel this. To say that hostilities had ceased, requires a proclamation to that effect by the highest executive authority, a proclamation that had not been made prior to the death of the insured, nor indeed at the time of the hearing of this cause. That such proclamation is the normal and usual procedure is found in the fact that since such hearing the President of the United States, on December 31, 1946, declared such hostilities to be ended, although it is still recognized that the United States continues to be in a state of war. As late as September 1, 1945, the President stated to the American people—

"It is not yet the day for the formal proclamation of the end of the war, or of the cessation of hostilities."

By numerous congressional enactments since the surrender of enemy armies, the Congress has recognized that this country was still "engaged in war," and as late as an act approved August 6, 1946, legislation was enacted which referred to "any war in which the United States is engaged on the date of the enactment of this section." Public Law 641, 79th Congress, Chapter 796, Second Session, H.R. 7039, 34 U.S.C.A. § 855c and note 5 U.S.C.A. § 797a. In the light of this generally accepted and recognized meaning of the term used in the policy under consideration, I cannot say that the parties to said insurance contract, or either of them, had any different understanding of the meaning of such provision. Whatever force there is to the contention of plaintiff that the provision under consideration is ambiguous exists, if at all, only as applied to a situation where the death of an insured in the military service of the United States and outside the "home areas" occurred after the declaration that hostilities have ended and before legislative or executive determination that the state of war is over, not to any time prior to the declaration by the President that hostilities have ceased. I cannot, therefore, say that such provision is ambiguous as applied to the instant case.

In this view, plaintiff's motion for summary judgment is denied, and defendant's motion for summary judgment is granted, with judgment, however, in favor of plaintiff for the "restricted amount" provided in the policy.

In reversing the *Stinson* decision of the lower court, the Court of Appeals established principles which were followed in several cases in 1948-1949. Five of the headnotes in this opinion related to the present subject:

> 7. *Constitutional law*
> Whether United States is engaged in war is a political question, determination of which rests with the legislative and executive branches of government, and their pronouncements are binding on the judiciary, from the standpoint of public law, but from the standpoint of private law different considerations are involved.
>
> 8. *War*
> The President's Proclamation fixing date of cessation of hostilities in World War II, was for public purposes, and does not necessarily apply to private contracts. Proclamation No. 2714, 50 U.S.C.A. Appendix, § 601 Note.
>
> 9. *Insurance*
> The phrase "cessation of hostilities," could not be interpolated in life policy restricting liability in case of death of insured in military or naval forces of country engaged in war.
>
> • • •
>
> 11. *War*
> The words "engaged in war" in common speech means actual warfare, terminated by capitulation of enemy forces.
>
> 12. *Insurance*
> Where insured was fatally injured when he fell from hotel window in France on October 2, 1945, while serving with occupation forces, the United States was not a country "engaged in war" within life policy provision restricting liability, even though war had not terminated in a political sense

Portions of the opinion are quoted below:

> The meaning of the phrase "engaged in war" may vary according to the purpose for which it was employed and the manner in which it was stated in relation to that purpose. The clause containing that phrase in the contract before us obviously purported to state a condition of non-liability for insurance coverage otherwise provided. The attempt was to define a period of non-liability, dependent on the military status of the insured and the war status of the country he served, by the use of relative terms, since it was impossible to forecast with definiteness the duration of that period.

[7] It is essential to note that fixation of the dates when (regarding World War II only, for the moment) this country became engaged in war and ceased, or will cease, to be engaged in war, depends entirely on the standpoint from which it is viewed.

[At pp. 236–237 the author cited relevant cases.]

Although appellee contends there is a "legal meaning" in the phrase "engaged in war", and that such meaning is commonly understood, the argument in support of that contention fails to disclose any specific act or pronouncement by one of the political departments which has marked or will mark the time when this country ceases to be engaged in war. By analogy to the several events occurring after the fact of surrender in World War I,[12*] which would qualify as political determination of the end of war within appellee's argument, apparently we are left to speculate on what act or pronouncement is sufficient to end this country's engagement in World War II.

The trial court said further, in the memorandum opinion, that "whatever force there is to the contention of plaintiff that the provision under consideration is ambiguous exists, if at all, only as applied to a situation where the death of an insured in the military service of the United States and outside the 'home areas' occurred after the declaration that hostilities have ended and before legislative or executive determination that the state of war is over, not to any time prior to the declaration by the President that hostilities have ceased. I cannot, therefore, say that such provision is ambiguous as applied to the instant case."

[8,9] We cannot agree with that statement, however. President Truman officially declared the cessation of hostilities in World War II "effective twelve o'clock noon, December 31, 1946,"[13*] but that proclamation was for public purposes, and didn't necessarily apply to private contracts. Even if it did, "cessation of hostilities" is not included in the language of this contract, nor can we interpolate such language.[14*]

• • •

[11,12] The insured was a layman who had entered active duty in the military service two years prior to the time this

---

*Footnotes 12-14 omitted

contract was executed. To the layman, and to the soldier, the words "engaged in war" convey the thought of actual warfare, terminated by capitulation of the enemy forces. The aftermath of actual warfare necessitates political and legal cognizance of a "state of war," but that is something apart from the common understanding of the time when the country ceases to be "engaged in war." President Truman's message to Congress,[15*] delivered September 6, 1945, epitomizes this difference in thinking, for early in his message he said, "The end of the war came more swiftly than most of us anticipated."[16*] Later, in the same message, when speaking of certain wartime statutes made effective "in time of war," "during the present war," or "for the duration of the war," he said, "The time has not yet arrived, however, for the proclamation of the cessation of hostilities, much less the termination of the war."[17*] And on November 11, 1918, President Wilson, in an address to Congress,[18*] read the terms of the armistice and declared: "The war thus comes to an end; for having accepted these terms of armistice, it will be impossible for the German command to renew it.[19*]

It can hardly be questioned that the spontaneous celebrations which occurred among the citizenry and troops of the victorious allied forces following announcement of the unconditional surrender by Japan were nothing more than exuberant jubilation occasioned by the commonly expressed thought that the war was over.

Appellee argues that the insured, as a reasonably intelligent man already in military service, can be presumed to have contemplated the necessity for the occupation of enemy lands, after the anticipated defeat of the enemy armies on the field of battle. That is a reasonable presumption, but appellee did not make it explicit, in the contract, that "engaged in war" included such consequential service. And we doubt, seriously, that any soldier considers occupation duty otherwise than as a consequence of war. "Engaged" and "war" have a meaning intimately related to actual warfare in the mind of a soldier, and while he may well contemplate occupation duty following the period of actual warfare, it requires no elaboration to point up his distinction of war and the consequential duty it may entail.

[At pp. 239-240 relevant cases are cited.]

---

*Footnotes 15-19 omitted.

In the light of the many adjudications subsequent to World War I, wherein it was held that ambiguous exemption clauses will be resolved in favor of the insured, that "engaged" and "war" are words which have been held to import various meanings, and that interpretation of such words will rest in common understanding in the absence of indicia that technical meaning was attached, it was particularly incumbent upon the insurer to make more obvious the meaning of the phrase "engaged in war" if it was to extend exemption past the time when enemy forces capitulated and actual warfare ceased. Otherwise the courts must imply that the insurer actually intended only to exclude liability during the continuation of the extraordinary risks incident to actual warfare, which defy actuarial prediction. An attempt, by the use of such a bald phrase, to escape from liability for death resulting from ordinary hazards, at a time when the extraordinary hazards no longer prevail, will seldom meet judicial condonation. We appreciate the fact that insurers face no small problem in framing exclusion clauses, but their draftmanship does not bear too onerous a burden to make more explicit, to the minds of laymen, the extent of the meaning of such a phrase as "engaged in war." We need not emphasize the ease with which ambiguity inherent in that phrase, in this manner of usage, could have been avoided.

It is interesting to observe that in a paper[24*] read before the section of Insurance Law, Illinois State Bar Association, March 20, 1946, an insurance counselor reviewed many war risk exclusion clause cases and noted that the question presented here was bound to arise. In surmising the result of the adjudication of this question he said[25*]: "It cannot be denied that if we apply the test such as used by the Supreme Court in the Aschenbrenner case[26] and assuming that the reference to war was not used in its technical sense but should be given the meaning which common speech imports, then the war must be deemed to have come to an end with the unconditional surrender of our enemies."

The conclusion we reach makes it unnecessary to determine whether the trial court committed error in sustaining the objection to appellant's interrogatories.

The judgment of the District Court is reversed and the case remanded for proceedings not inconsistent with this opinion.

Reversed and remanded.

---

*Footnotes 24-25 omitted.

[26]292 U.S. 80 (1934). Remainder of footnote 26 omitted.

The opinions in the cases following *Stinson* to a large extent repeated the principles set forth in that case. Rather than quoting from the opinions in the later cases, the relevant headnotes are quoted as summaries:

New York Life Ins. Co. v. Durham[11]; the Circuit Court of Appeals, Tenth Circuit

1. *Constitutional Law*
The existence of war and restoration of peace are determined solely by political departments of government and such determinations are conclusively binding on courts in all matters of state or public concern, and war having been declared, its existence must be recognized by courts until peace is proclaimed, although actual warfare may have ceased.

2. *War*
In determining judicial questions concerning commencement or termination of a state of war, courts are generally required to refer to some public act of the political department of the government.

3. *War*
Private rights, when affected by the incidence of war, are governed by determinations of political departments of government, and courts will usually condition private rights, whether resting in contract or otherwise, in order to give full effect to the exigencies of war.

4. *Contracts*
In all private matters, unaffected by public interest, parties are free to contract with reference to war and to give to it such definition, connotation and meaning as does not infringe upon public policy.

5. *Insurance*
Insured and insurer were free to contract with reference to a "country engaged in war" as a measure of liability, and courts must construe that term according to manifest intent of the parties.

6. *Insurance*
Where life policy restricted liability if death of insured occurred outside home areas while in military or naval forces of country engaged in war including undeclared war, the parties used the word "war" not in its technical or formal sense, but rather in practical and realistic sense in which it is commonly used, in the sense it bears to the hazards to human life.

7. *Insurance*

Where insured died while in military forces of United States outside home areas from wholly non-military causes after unconditional surrender of enemies, but before declaration announcing formal termination of existence of a state of war, he was not in service of "country engaged in war" within clause of life policy restricting liability.

Trimble v. Western and Southern Life Ins. Co.[12]; Court of Appeals of Ohio, Butler County

1. *Insurance*

War clause in life policy excepting liability for accidental death during service of insured in military forces of a country at war or in time of war was not void as contravening public policy.

2. *Insurance*

War clause in life policy excepting liability for accidental death during service of insured in military forces of a country at war or in time of war makes mere status of insured as a member of armed forces sufficient to make clause operative.

3. *Evidence*

Court of Appeals took judicial notice of a state of war existing between United States and Japan, which actually was not terminated by ceremonies aboard battleship Missouri on September 2, 1945, but was followed with active hostilities in a different theater of action thereafter.

4. *Insurance*

War clause in life policy excepting liability for accidental death during service of insured in military forces of a country at war or in time of war was unambiguous and permitted of no construction other than to give effect to plain language without contradiction.

National Life and Accident Ins. Co. Inc. v. Leverett[13]; Court of Appeals of Texas

8. *Insurance*

Where, at time of death of insured, a recruiting officer, on June 18, 1947, there had been no treaty of peace signed with Germany or Japan, but there was no state of war existing with Germany or Japan, provision of life policy that double indemnity should be automatically suspended during time insured was enrolled in military service in time of "war" was not applicable in action by beneficiary to recover double indemnity.

Mutual Life Ins. Co. of New York v. Davis[14]; Court of Appeals of Georgia

1. *Evidence*
Courts will take judicial notice of beginning, existence and ending of all wars in which United States has participated.

2. *Evidence*
Court of Appeals took judicial notice that World War II terminated on date of unconditional surrender of Japan on August 15, 1945.

3. *Evidence*
Allegation of a petition which negative facts, the truth of which a court must take judicial cogizance, must be disregarded.

4. *Insurance*
An insurance policy is a simple contract, the provisions of which should be construed as any other type of contract.

5. *Contracts*
Construction of an unambiguous contract is a question of law for the court and cardinal rule for construction is to ascertain the intention of the parties. Code, § § 20-701, 20-702.

6. *Insurance*
Life policy precluding double indemnity recovery if death of insured resulted from "military or naval service in time of war" or from any act incident thereto manifested intention to relieve insurer from double indemnity liability while insured was engaged in hazardous occupation of military or naval service in time of war in event he met his death as direct result thereto or as direct result of an act incident to war, and such clause was inapplicable to preclude recovery after unconditional surrender of Japan.

7. *Insurance*
In order for a happening to be an "act incident to war" within meaning of military or naval service exception clause of double indemnity provision of life policy, there must have been a war in existence at time of such happening.

8. *Insurance*
Army officer who was killed as result of explosion of an ammunition dump in Germany on August 19, 1945, or 4 days after surrender of Japan, was not killed in time of "war" within meaning of provision in life policy excluding recovery of double indemnity if death of insured resulted from military or naval service in time of war or from any "act incident to war."

Attention is called to *Darnall v. Day*[15] decided by the Supreme Court of Iowa in 1949, even though it was not a life insurance case. Citing *Stinson* and *Durham,* the Court held that "war," in the practical and realistic sense in which it is commonly understood, refers to the period of hostilities and not to a technical state of war which may exist after the fighting has ended. Four justices concurred in the majority decision on this point. Two justices dissented on other points. *Darnall v. Day* was cited in later insurance cases.

Notes

1. 25 S.E. 2d 475 (1943); 202 S.C. 422 (1943).
2. 145 P. 2d 227 (1944); 65 Idaho 408 (1944).
3. 67 U.S. (2 Black) 635 (1862).
4. 136 F. 445 (1905).
5. 57 F. Supp. 620 (1944).
6. 37 Hawaiian Reports 208 (1945).
7. *Stankus v. New York Life Ins. Co.* 44 N.E. 2d 687 (1942); 312 Mass. 366 (1942).
8. 158 F. 2d 260 (1946), rehearing denied; cert. denied, 331 U.S. 811 (1946); rehearing denied, 331 U.S. 867 (1946).
9. 67 C.J. Sec. 1 on War.
10. 69 F. Supp. 860 (1947); 167 F. 2d 233 (1948).
11. 166 F. 2d 874 (1948).
12. 82 N.E. 2d 548 (1948).
13. 215 S.W. 2d 939 (1948).
14. 53 S.E. 2d 571 (1949); 79 Ga. App. 336.
15. 37 N.W. 2d 277 (1949); 240 Iowa 665 (1949).

2

THE CONFLICT IN KOREA

1. *Early Cases (1952-1953) Holding the Conflict Not a War*

The first important case (and almost certainly the first case) involving the effects of the conflict in Korea on the provisions of a life insurance contract was tried in the County Court of Allegheny County, Pennsylvania in 1951. The court in *Beley v. Pennsylvania Mut. Life Ins. Co.*[1] held that the conflict was "war." The decision was reversed by the Pennsylvania Superior Court, which denied rehearing; the Supreme Court of Pennsylvania affirmed the Superior Court's judgment; and the U.S. Supreme Court denied certiorari. Thus, the final decision was that the Korean conflict was not "war" for purposes of determining liability under a life insurance policy.

A similar case was tried and decided at the same time—*Harding v. Pennsylvania Mut. Life Ins. Co.*[2]—with a history and results like those of *Beley*.

The opinions of the different courts in *Beley* and *Harding* were not identical, even though the decisions concerning the definition of "war" were the same.

The opinion of the Superior Court in *Harding* contained more detail on such definition than did *Beley*, and the following quotations are taken from *Harding*. The quoted headnotes constitute a summary of the Court's unanimous decision:

> 1. *Insurance*
> Where, on December 31, 1946, the President had issued proclamation declaring hostilities to have terminated, and Congress, on July 25, 1947, officially declared end of World War II, for purpose of risk assumed under life policy, the war with the Axis Powers had ended. Pa.R.C.P. No. 1034, 12 P.S. Appendix.

2. *Constitutional Law*

The existence of war and restoration of peace is determined by political departments of government, and such determinations are conclusive upon the courts in all matters of state or public concern, but, in all private matters, unaffected by public interest, the parties are free to contract with reference to war and to give it such definition, connotation, and meaning as does not infringe upon public policy. 26 U.S. C.A. § 22(b) (13).

3. *Evidence*

Until proper department of government determines that a war exists, the courts cannot take judicial notice thereof. 26 U.S.C.A. § 22(b) (13).

4. *Insurance*

Term "war" in life policy which provided that double indemnity provision would be inapplicable if death resulted from or if insured engaged in military, air, or naval service in time of war was susceptible of more than one construction since it failed to distinguish between declared and undeclared war, and, therefore, term would be construed in favor of insured and against insurer. Pa. R.C.P. No. 1034, 12 P.S. Appendix; 26 U.S.C.A. § 22(b) (13).

5. *Insurance*

In action on life policy, which was issued one month after commencement of hostilities in Korea, and in which term "war" as used in provision making double indemnity provision inapplicable was ambiguous, insurer had burden to establish that term applied to undeclared as well as declared war, and insurer failed to meet this burden. Pa. R.C.P. No. 1034, 12 P.S. Appendix; 26 U.S.C.A. § 22(b) (13).

6. *War and National Defense*

"War", in law, is not a mere contest of physical force, on however large a scale.

7. *Insurance*

Words and phrases in an insurance contract are used and intended to be used in their legal sense.

8. *Contracts*

A contract phrase, if susceptible of two interpretations, must be given that which accords with settled law.

9. *Contracts*

Where the law gives to certain words an established meaning, this meaning is less readily controlled by the standard of interpretation otherwise applicable than is the meaning of other words.

Relevant portions of the Court's opinion are quoted below:

[1] . . .

We now come to the second and crucial phase of appellee's argument, to wit, that the United States was at war with Korea at the time of the insured's induction into federal service. Not only is the question one of first impression in this Commonwealth, but so far as we have been able to discover, both by our own and counsel's diligent and exhaustive research, the question has not heretofore been raised in the reported decision of any appellate court, either federal or state. The nearest approach to it is in Youngstown Sheet and Tube Co. v. Sawyer, and Sawyer v. Youngstown Sheet and Tube Co., 72 S. Ct. 863, the so-called "Steel Seizure Cases" in the United States Supreme Court.

[quotation omitted]

[2] Since there appears to be general agreement that the conflict in Korea is not declared war, our next and final step is to determine whether it is undeclared war. That there is a marked distinction between the two was first pointed out in Bas v. Tingy, 4 Dall. 37, 4 U.S. 37, 1 L.Ed. 731, and most recently in New York Life Ins. Co. v. Durham, 10 Cir., 166 F.2d 874, 875. In that case the New York Life Insurance Company issued its policy of insurance on the life of Lewis Durham, conditioned that the amount payable would be the restricted amount (as therein defined) if the death of the insured should occur "while *** in the military *** forces of any country engaged in war. *** '[W]ar' includes undeclared war." As stated in the opinion of the Court, 166 F.2d at pages 875, 876:

> "*** The existence of war and restoration of peace are determined *** by the political departments of our Government, and such determinations are conclusively binding upon the Courts in all matters of *state or public* concern ***. *But in all private matters, unaffected by public interest, the parties are undoubtedly free to contract with reference to war and to give it such definition, connotation and meaning, as does not infringe upon public policy.* [Citing cases.] See cases collected in Annotation 168 A.L.R. 685. ***
>
> "The parties in this case *** contracted with reference to a risk assumed for a premium paid. When they came to

express the limitations upon the risk assumed, they obviously had in mind the extraordinary risk incident to service in the military forces of any country engaged in war, *declared or undeclared.* By including undeclared war, they chose not to use the word 'war' in its technical or formal sense, but rather in the practical and realistic sense in which it is commonly used and understood—in the sense it bears to the hazards to human life. The parties clearly contemplated that the country might be engaged in an undeclared war, without political determination or formal recognition thereof, yet the Courts would be required to take cognizance of its existence by an appraisal of actualities in order to give legal effect to the insurance contract." (Emphasis added.)

If that is what the parties in the case at bar contemplated, why did they not make clear their intention by including undeclared war, as was done in the Durham case and in Stinson v. New York Life Ins. Co., 83 U.S. App. D.C. 115, 167 F.2d 233. In the Stinson case the policy stated, 167 F.2d at page 234, that "'Wherever used in this Policy, *** "War" includes undeclared war'"; and 167 F.2d on page 236 the Court said, referring to Citizens Protective League v. Clark, 81 U.S. App. D.C. 116, 155 F.2d 290: "In the Clark case we were treating a matter of public law [Enemy Alien Act]; here we are concerned with a private contract, and a distinction must be maintained."

The case for the appellee has been ably presented but we have not been furnished with, nor have we been able to find, a direct precedent, either legal or factual, for the action of the President of the United States in dispatching troops to Korea.

• • •

[3] We are not here concerned with the constitutional authority of the President to dispatch troops to Korea to repel the armed aggression against the Republic of Korea, generally conceded to be in pursuance to and under the authority of article 39 of the United Nations Charter.[4*] Our concern is whether the nation has thereby been committed to an undeclared war of which we must take judicial notice. "*The courts are bound by a declaration or determination by the proper department of government that a war exists, while until there has been such a declaration or determination the courts cannot take judicial notice of the existence of a war by their government*". 67 C.J.

---

*Footnote 4 omitted.**

336. (Emphasis added.) Cited to the text is Bishop v. Jones & Petty, 28 Tex. 294, to which we shall later refer in more detail. And on page 338, after stating that war may commence or exist without a declaration on either side, it is said that "*A court cannot, however, take judicial notice of a war by its government until there has been some act or declaration creating or recognizing the existence of war by the department of government clothed with the war-making power.*" (Emphasis added.)
[Earlier cases in support were reviewed, with quotation from *Bennion,* and cases *pro* and *contra* were cited.]

[4] Since there is a valid distinction between declared and undeclared war, which has been recognized by insurance companies, notably the New York Life Insurance Company, in drawing up contracts of insurance especially since Pearl Harbor, the use of the term "war" in the contract under consideration presents an ambiguity. That being the case, the cardinal rule of construction, that where a policy is susceptible of more than one construction it must be liberally construed in favor of the insured and against the insurer, is so universally and firmly established as to no longer require citation.

[*Palmetto* and *Stinson* were cited in support.]

[5] Since "war" is a word which has been held to import various meanings, it is incumbent upon the insurer to make clear that it applies to undeclared war, as well as to declared war, for even if the action in Korea should be held to be war, it is at most an undeclared war. In our opinion the insurer has failed to meet the burden cast upon it. The attempt of the appellee to evade liability of double indemnity should not receive judicial condonation. The phraseology of the policy was chosen by the insurer and tendered in fixed form to the prospective policyholder, and since its language is reasonably open to two constructions, we will adopt that construction which is more favorable to the insured.

• • •

[6] The attack on the Republic of Korea has been likened to the Japanese attack on Pearl Harbor, but the aggression which we are seeking to repel in Korea has an entirely different status than the attack upon our fleet and other armed forces at Pearl Harbor. That constituted a direct attack upon the United States but, according to the weight of authority, war with Japan did not begin until the next day, following the declaration by Congress. We are not unmindful of the extent of the hostilities and

the casualties we have suffered from the action in Korea, but as stated in Vol. 44 Words and Phrases, page 624, " 'War' in law, is not a mere contest of physical force, on however large a scale."

[7-9] As ably stated in Rosenau v. Idaho Mutual Benefit Ass'n, supra, 65 Idaho 408, 145 P.2d 227, 230: "*** we are here concerned with the meaning and intent of the word [war] as contained in a formal, legal contract of insurance, a class of contracts which the courts are very frequently called upon to consider and construe, and it seems quite obvious that words and phrases in a contract of this nature, are used and intended to be used in the legal sense. The rule applicable here is stated in 17 C.J.S., Contracts, § 300, page 717, as follows: 'A phrase in a contract, if susceptible of two interpretations, must be given that according with settled law. Where the law gives to certain words an established meaning, this meaning is less readily controlled by the standard of interpretation otherwise applicable than is the meaning of other words.' "

Judgment reversed and here entered for the plaintiff for the full amount of the policy.

The Pennsylvania Supreme Court upheld the Superior Court's decision in *Harding*, citing *Beley* in which an opinion had been handed down on the same day. The Chief Justice and three justices joined in the *Harding* decision, with two justices dissenting for the reasons which they set forth in their dissenting opinions in *Beley*. The Supreme Court of the United States denied certiorari.

Turning to *Beley*, the opinion of the Superior Court was brief since, as the Court stated, it did not differ in any essential respect from *Harding*. As in the Pennsylvania Supreme Court decision in *Harding*, three justices joined with the Chief Justice in the majority decision and two justices dissented. The Supreme Court of the United States denied certiorari.

A review of the Pennsylvania Supreme Court opinions in *Beley* (majority, dissenting and concurring) follows:

1. *Insurance*

Under life policy provisions that limited insurer's liability under principal insuring clause to return of premiums paid if insured engaged in military service in time of war and made double indemnity provision inapplicable if insured's death resulted from military service in time of war or work in connection with actual warfare or police duties, insurer was liable although insured was killed in action in Korea while serving with United States Army infantry, which was a contingent of United Nations forces. Mutual Defense Assistance Act of 1949, § 1 et seq., 22 U.S.C.A. § 1571 et seq.; Joint Resolution July 25, 1947, § 4, 50 U.S.C.A. Appendix, § 584 note.

2. *War and National Defense*

The action being waged in Korea is not a "war" within what may be termed the constitutional or legal sense of that word. Mutual Defense Assistance Act of 1949, § 1 et seq., 22 U.S.C.A. § 1571 et seq.; Joint Resolution July 25, 1947, § 4, 50 U.S.C.A. Appendix, § 584 note.

3. *Insurance*

The right of an insured to recover under a life policy should not be left to depend upon determination of a question not governable by definite test either legal or factual but its terms and conditions should be interpreted according to some definite and uniform standard.

4. *Insurance*

If meaning of any term of a policy is in doubt, that doubt should be resolved in favor of insured.

5. *Insurance*

In interpreting life policy, it would be assumed that if insurer had meant to invest term "war" with a broader connotation than its constitutional or legal intendment, insurer would have effected this by addition of words indicating such intentions. Mutual Defense Assistance Act of 1949, § 1 et seq., 22 U.S.C.A. § 1571 et seq.; Joint Resolution July 25, 1947, § 4, 50 U.S.C.A. Appendix, § 584 note.

6. *Constitutional Law*

The existence or nonexistence of a "state of war" is a political, not a judicial, question, and it is only if and when a formal declaration of war has been made by political department of government that judicial cognizance may be taken thereof, and that such determination becomes binding upon the judiciary.

• • •

Opinion: Horace Stern, Chief Justice

Is the present struggle in Korea a "war" within the meaning of that term as employed in a certain life insurance policy? That is the question for decision in this litigation.

• • •

The opinion summarized the actions of Congress, the President and the Security Council of the United Nations which had authorized the presence of American forces acting as a contingent of United Nations' forces in Korea.

[2] Although Congress has, in certain enactments, recognized that military forces of the United States are operating in Korea and has appropriated funds for the support of the armed forces there, it is obvious from the above recital of events that there was not, nor ever has been, any declaration of war by Congress against any other country, state or nation, but merely a dispatch to Korea by Presidential order of military, naval and air forces of the United States in accordance with the provisions of the Charter of the United Nations and the recommendations of the Security Council. Since, therefore, it is Congress that has the power under the Constitution to declare war, and since that power is exclusive, Youngstown Sheet & Tube Co. v. Sawyer, 343 U.S. 579, 642, 72 S.Ct. 863, 96 L.Ed. 1153, it is clear that the action being waged in Korea is not a "war" within what may be termed the "constitutional" or "legal" sense of that term. Defendant urges, however, that it is in *fact* a war, because what started apparently as a minor "police action" has developed, by reason of its duration, its bitterness, and the number of its casualties, into a sanguinary struggle of grave proportions, and urges further that the connotation of the word "war" in the Company's insurance policies should not be limited to a formally declared war, but embraces any clash of arms in which the methods of war are pursued, and especially where the conflict is, as in Korea, of such extensive dimensions. The trouble with this argument is that if the word "war" in such policies were to be interpreted as other than one declared by Congress, courts would be utterly at sea whenever the question arose as to whether certain expeditions in which United States forces were engaged constituted a war. It has been pointed out in a report of the Committee on Foreign Affairs of the House of Representatives that during the period between 1798 and 1945 there were some 150 or more occasions on which our military forces were engaged in various countries, notably in China, Mexico, Central American

and Caribbean Republics, in the course of some of which incidents there were really serious engagements and many casualties. Who, then, would be the tribunal to decide whether such an undeclared conflict did or did not amount to a "war,"—a jury, a court? What would be the criterion of decision,—the number of troops involved, the number of casualties, the duration of the hostilities? If, for example, Beley had lost his life in action in Korea a day or two after our troops first arrived there, would a war have then existed, or would it not have become a war until the magnitude of the struggle finally revealed itself and the casualty lists became so distressingly long and frequent?

[3-5] Obviously the right of an insured to recover under a life insurance policy should not be left to depend upon the determination of a question not governable by any definite test either legal or factual; on the contrary, its terms and conditions should be interpreted according to some definite and uniform standard. Even were it to be conceded that the meaning of any of its terms was really involved in doubt, that doubt, according to all established canons of construction, should be resolved in favor of the insured. A policy of life insurance is a highly technical instrument, drawn up presumably with meticulous care by legal experts on behalf of the Insurance Company, and who not only intend to use all terms in their legal sense but know how to accomplish that result; it may be assumed, therefore, that if defendant had here meant to invest the term "war" with a broader connotation than its "constitutional" or "legal" intendment, it would have effected this by the addition of words indicating such an intention as, for example, "declared or undeclared" war.

[6] The existence or nonexistence of a state of war is a political, not a judicial, question, and it is only if and when a formal declaration of war has been made by the political department of the government that judicial cognizance may be taken thereof; when so made it becomes binding upon the judiciary. Bishop v. Jones & Petty, 28 Tex. 294, 319, 320; Perkins v. Rogers, 35 Ind. 124, 167; Hamilton v. McClaughry, C.C., 136 F. 445, 449; Verano v. DeAngelis Coal Co., D.C., 41 F. Supp. 954. An exact question involving the application of this principle arose in connection with the Japanese surprise attack on Pearl Harbor on December 7, 1941, war with Japan not being officially declared by Congress until the day following, December 8. As we all know, an appalling number of lives were lost in that infamous attack, and yet, in a majority of the cases involving the interpretation of the word "war" as employed in life insurance policies similar to the one here in question, it was

held that war did not exist on December 7, and therefore the beneficiaries of such policies were entitled to recover. West v. Palmetto State Life Insurance Co., 202 S.C. 422, 25 S.E.2d 475, 145 A.L.R. 1461; Rosenau v. Idaho Mutual Benefit Association, 65 Idaho 408, 145 P.2d 227; Savage v. Sun Life Assurance Co. of Canada, D.C., 57 F. Supp. 620; Pang v. Sun Life Assurance Co. of Canada, 37 Haw. 208, 14 C.C.H. Life Cases 496.

• • •

The judgment of the Superior Court is affirmed.

CHIDSEY, Justice (dissenting).

I agree with the majority that the disposition of this case depends upon the meaning to be given the word "war" in the policy of insurance involved, but I disagree with their interpretation. The likelihood of death occurring and the consequent increase in the risk assumed by the insurer if any insured voluntarily or involuntarily engages in military service in time of war, is manifest. The exclusion or termination of liability of the insurer in such event is therefore founded upon good reason, readily understandable by both parties to the insurance contract. The greater likelihood of an insured's death when engaged in military service in time of war exists whether the war is a declared or "constitutional" war, or an undeclared war. The reason for the exclusion applies equally in either instance. The word "war" used without limitation or restriction, in my opinion should be construed as the word would ordinarily be used and understood and calls for no technical construction. Certainly a major conflict between the armed forces of two nations under authority of their respective governments would be commonly regarded as war. I think that the present conflict in Korea is a war within the meaning of the exclusionary provisions of the policy, and therefore dissent from the view of the majority.

BELL, Justice (dissenting).

• • •

Although learned and distinguished Judges have allowed a recovery under this policy, their decision seems to me incomprehensible. The majority, I believe, ignore all the other language, terms and conditions of the policy—which are insuperable barriers to recovery—and pin their decision on one word "war". They hold that the Korean War is not War. This will shock millions and millions of American citizens and especially Korean veterans and their families. Every man, woman and child in America is informed by the newspapers and radio and knows that there are many thousands of American soldiers, sailors, marines and airmen who are now and for several years have been engaged with soldiers of North Korea and of China in open actual warfare. Our Navy is constantly patrolling and bombarding the coasts of North Korea; our Air Force is having daily dog fights with the enemy, and our soldiers are daily killing the enemy and being killed. We have for over two years been engaged in negotiations for truce and are vainly trying *to exchange prisoners of war.* The United States casualties exceed 128,000. How is it humanly possible to say that the Korean War is not war? Moreover, even if the majority's construction of that one word "war" were correct, it does not meet or answer, as we shall see, the other pertinent provisions of the policy which prohibit recovery.

The parties to a private contract, unaffected by a public interest, can make any agreement they wish (unless it is against public policy). The question therefore is: What did this private contract insure against? The majority change and *limit* the policy to read "if death shall result by reason of military service in war"; and then hold that the word "war" means a "Constitutional" war; and the Korean War is not a Constitutionally declared war. A reading of the policy will quickly demonstrate that the risk it covered, paid for and insured against, covered and was intended to cover peacetime activities in contradistinction to wartime activities.

The greater likelihood of death occurring, and the consequent increase in the risk assumed by the Insurance Company if the insured engaged in military service in time of war, is manifest; and it would seem obvious that the premium or cost would undoubtedly be much larger if the risk included death from war than if it only included death from peacetime activities. It is likewise obvious that the risk or likelihood of death would be equally great whether the insured was engaged in military service in time of actual war or in time of a "constitutionally declared" war; and consequently the line of distinction or demarcation which the majority seek to draw has no basis, reason or logic to support it.

Was this *"an accidental death"*; did death result from "military service *in time of war*"; or if not, did death result from work in connection with *"actual warfare"*; or if not did death result from *"intentional injuries inflicted by another person"*; or if not, what did death result from? The majority's only attempt to answer these questions is to discuss the word "war".

It is well settled that ordinary words are to be given their ordinary and generally understood meaning, unless the instrument itself, considered in the light of the surrounding circumstances, clearly shows them to have been used in a technical or different sense. "The standard for the interpretation of words is their natural meaning to the parties who have contracted at the time and place where the contract is made, considering all the circumstances surrounding it."

• • •

Plaintiff in order to recover must therefore prove (1) that death was "*accidental*" and (2) that death did not result (a) from military service "*in time of war*", or (b) from "*actual warfare*", or (c) from "*intentional injuries inflicted by another person*", as these terms are ordinarily understood and accepted.

It is said that there have been 156 armed fightings in the history of our Country. Some of these have been wars, some not; each case depends upon its own particular facts. In this case the mere fact that President Truman has declared the Korean War to be a "police action" does not, irrespective of his motives, make it so in construing a private contract of insurance.[1*]

Although for political or international reasons, or to save the "position" of their leader, the majority in Congress have not formally declared war against the North Koreans or Red China, *the Congress* (as well as every person in the civilized world) *knows that the United States* is at war in Korea. See for example, the Veterans' Readjustment Assistance Act of 1952, Public Law 550, U.S. Code Congressional and Administrative News 1952, pp. 629-655, 38 U.S.C.A. § 901 et seq.; and the 1952 Amendment to the Veterans' Compensation Rates statute, Public Law 427, U.S. Code Congressional and Administrative News 1952, p. 290, 38 U.S.C.A. §§ 473, 478, 480, Veterans' Regulation No. 1(a), pt. 1, par. 2. In the legislative history of the

---

[*1]Moreover, if contrary to the belief of countless millions of American citizens, the Korean War is not war but only "a police action" as President Truman and his administration say, does it not follow that a soldier killed therein was performing "*police duties* or any act incidental thereto, either on land or water", and hence cannot recover under the express terms of the policy!

Veterans' Compensation Rates statute of 1952 it is said, pages 1784-1785: "Your committee *** believes that the bill, as amended, will provide uniformity for *veterans of all wars* insofar as it deals with statutory awards for the more seriously disabled groups. *** All the provisions of this bill apply entirely and exclusively to service connected veterans of the Spanish-American War Group, World Wars 1 and 2 and veterans of service on or after June 27, 1950." (Date of Korean conflict.)

Congress has also made provision for the use of United States troops in Korea by making appropriations totaling billions of dollars, Public Law 843, 81st Congress, Supplemental Appropriation Act of 1951, 64 Stat. 1054. Furthermore, the Revenue Act of 1950 provides for certain income tax exemptions for members of the Armed Forces serving in combat zones, Korea being, of course, in this category. Public Law § 814, 81st Congress, § 202, 26 U.S.C.A. §§ 22(b) (13), 1621(a) 1625(a), 1633 (a). But all of this deals with political questions and with issues arising thereout; it does not deal with private contracts and their meaning and intent.

[Cases in support of this position were cited—*Stankus v. New York Life Insurance Co.*; *Bas v. Tingy*; *the Steel Seizure case*; *New York Life Insurance Co., v. Bennion*; *Mutual Life Insurance Co. v. Davis*; *the Prize Cases*; and cases defining "accidental death."]

These limitations clearly define and illuminate and limit the intentions of the parties and create and constitute insuperable barriers to a recovery under the facts of this case!

For each of these reasons I would affirm the judgment of the Court of Common Pleas.

Justice Musmanno's Opinion Concurring with the Majority

• • •

In discussing the principles of law involved in this case, we must assert at once that to deny that the Korean military action is not war in its popularly accepted meaning is to deny the evidence of one's senses. Courts normally take judicial notice of whatever is unquestioningly accepted by informed society as fact. A judge does not ask in court for proof that ice forms at the North Pole or that the World Series refers to a contest between baseball teams. Courts know that in Korea, armies are pitted against each other utilizing every device known to modern warfare in the effort and determination to exterminate each other. We know this to be true because every medium of communication extant informs us that it is true. There is not one voice, one printed word, or one picture in the newspapers, radio broadcasts and television images which present themselves before our eyes or appeal to our ears that bespeaks anything to the contrary. In addition, judges have physically seen soldiers who have returned from Korea and have witnessed the evidence of their contact with forces which have inflicted wounds peculiarly the result of gunfire and cannon fire, the trademark of war.

Judges have seen, through the media of incontestible authenticity, photographic evidence of flag-draped caskets being returned by ship from the distant peninsula of Korea. Figures released by the United States Government, through official reports which the courts accept unless controverted (and there has been no denial anywhere of their accuracy), establish that our casualties in Korea have reached the dreadful total of more than 128,000, of which 22,519 represents deaths. Nothing can more graphically identify conflict as war than grave casualties of this awesome character.

And yet, the Spanish American war, which is accepted governmentally and historically and in every other manner as a full-scale war, produced the *relatively* small number of 361 battle deaths and 2,565 deaths by disease. The total casualties reached, again *comparatively*, the small number of 4,506. The number of American troops engaged was 306,760.

However, even the loss of one life or none at all, if there be a solemn declaration of war, makes any military action, war. Congress is the only body in the United States which can declare war. The Korea conflict is non-congressionally declared war. Does that in itself make it legally different from congressionally declared war? The answer to that question is the answer to the question posed in this lawsuit.

> [The Justice cited and quoted from *Bas v. Tingy; Bishop v. Jones & Petty*; *67 Corpus Juris 336*; and *Report No. 127*, Committee on Foreign Affairs, House of Representatives (1951).]

If the drafters of the contract of insurance which was sold to the plaintiff here intended the word War used therein to be interpreted in its constitutional sense, the plaintiff is entitled to recover, since the action which brought about the death of Andrew Beley was not within the purport of the exclusionary clause. The task of the judiciary in this case has been not to define the word War in its broad general application but what it was intended to mean by the parties to the contract, in the light of the history and the circumstances of the time.

The word War has many meanings. In addition to being an armed conflict, it may be defined as an act of opposition, as an inimical contest, as hostility and strife. It may have a locale not ordinarily associated with its gunpowder connotation, as, for instance, Milton speaks of "impious *war* in heaven," and in Psalms (lv. 21) we find: "The words of his mouth were smoother than butter but *war* was in his heart." The word War may take on still further meanings when conjoined to another word which has acquired a particular significance because of the history of the times. Thus, the phrase Cold War has painted a canvas of dramatic and tragic scope and depth beyond the capacity of imagination a decade ago.

The question presented by this case has not definitively been passed upon, so far as research can ascertain, by any court of last resort in the United States. However, various decisions have lifted lanterns of light on the seeming paradoxical query as to whether the conflict in Korea is War or not. The decision in the case of New York Life Insurance Co. v. Durham, 10 Cir. 166 F.2d 874, 875, sheds its own particular beam of analysis on the subject.

[The definitions of "war" in the opinions rendered in the lower court and in the Circuit Court of Appeals, Tenth Circuit, were cited and discussed. The Justice stated, in part:]

. . . the adjudication of the rights of the contending parties cannot be ascertained through the process of conjecture or chance. The insurance company, whose attorneys wrote the contract, must stand by the words employed by their agents; and in this connection War, in the contemplation of the law of the United States, can only mean war declared by the only authority that can declare it, i.e., Congress.

If we were to denominate as war all foreign actions in which United States military forces have been engaged, we would have to conclude that the United States has practically never been at peace in the history of our country. From 1798 to 1952 the United States has used armed forces abroad some 150 times.[1*] Some of these actions, of course, involved no casualties but many of them did. But it is not the number of casualties which decides whether or not a foreign military action is a

---

*1 *House Report No. 127*, pp. 55-62.

"legal" war or not. No one would have seriously contended that the slight commitments of American troops on June 27, 1950, to the Korean action constituted war. Nor would authorities on international law have declared that the American action in Korea a month later constituted war. If the Korean action was not war on June 27 or July 27, when did it become war? Five months later? A year later? When?

Would the appellant insurance company argue that the military action became war when the casualties reached a certain figure, say 5,000 or 10,000? Would it argue that the action certainly was war when the casualties mounted to 50,000? And if we assume that a certain degree on the metamorphical thermometer of casualties marked the point at which the military action became war, who would determine when that point was reached? The courts certainly could not declare that point of demarcation, and there is no law which provides for such an arbitrary determination of what constitutes war. Nor could it be argued successfully that a military action becomes war when a certain period of time has elapsed, since there is no constitutional or statutory basis for such an automatic chronological determination. The courts interpret law and construe facts; they cannot *make* facts, and that is what, in effect, the appellant would have us do by asking that we decide when the military action in Korea passed from a military action into a legal or constitutional war.

If the logic of the appellant insurance company were to be accepted in application to history, then the Pershing Punitive Expedition into Mexico, the Boxer Expedition into China, the many Nicaraguan Marine expeditions and others of that character, all involving American casualties, would have to be regarded as wars. But no historian would agree with such a conclusion.

There can be acts of war without there being a state of war. Beley was killed by an act of war but not in a state of war. The case of New York Life Insurance Co. v. Bennion, 10 Cir., 158 F.2d 260, 261, is illustrative of this proposition.

[The opinion continued with discussion of *Bennion, Durham, Harding,* and *West v. Palmetto,* with this conclusion:]

It can only be assumed in the case at bar that the parties accepted the insurance contract in May, 1945, "in contemplation of the law of the United States under which only Congress can declare war."

If the Beley insurance contract had included the phrase "undeclared war," which the Korean conflict indubitably is, no problem would have arisen because the Korean conflict, in the constitutional sense, indubitably is an undeclared war. However, since that phrase does not appear in the contract, we are compelled to unclasp the book of history of 1945 and scan the pages of the times immediately preceding and surrounding the writing of the contract.

[As a background for establishment of the relationship between the United States and the United Nations, the opinion contained a historical summary. The Justice concluded:]

Americans generally believed in 1945 that the blossomtime of Hope had arrived, and that the Four Horsemen of the Apocalypse would never again gallop their martial steeds across the bleeding face of the earth. We had reason to believe that with the world assembled in the Parliament of Man, the war clause in our own Constitution could conceivably gradually become obsolete. Expeditionary missions there would be; the enforcement of the decisions of the United Nations would entail the commitment of groups of our armed forces, together with those of other nations, to remote crossroads on the globe, but full-scaled wars—with the United States alone on one side and another or other nations on the other side—was a possibility that we believed was melting rapidly in the crucible of international amity.

It was against that background of general understanding (whether the drafters of the Beley insurance policy consciously realized it or not) that the contract here before us was written. And it may well be that, because of our responsibilities under the Charter of the United Nations, Congress will never be called upon again to declare war in its originally accepted significance. According to Article 39, supra, the Security Council "shall determine the existence of any threat to the peace, breach of the peace, or act of aggression and shall make recommendations". Since defensive war on our part could only come about through aggression against us (which subject matter is now in the exclusive hands of the United Nations) and since we would never wage an aggressive war ourselves, it is exceedingly problematical that there ever would be another occasion for Congress to declare war except merely to confirm action already agreed upon by the United Nations.

It might be that, in this new state of affairs, an amendment to the Constitution will be in order to assign to Congress the sole power to determine when our military forces are to be used in implementing a decision of the United Nations Security Council. Obviously, under present constitutional interpretation superimposed over current international obligations, the President can commit our armed forces into military actions on a scale which can equal and even surpass in magnitude the congressionally declared wars of the past. Whether the people of the nation desire that this shall remain a fixed attribute of the executive power of government, thus vitally curtailing the powers of the legislative branch of our government, is a matter for serious concern. However, this is simply an observation of the writer not needed to the adjudication of this case.

From all the above, I conclude that Andrew Beley did not come to his death as the result of a state of War as contemplated by the contracting parties and that, therefore, the plaintiff is entitled to recover the full value of the policy.

I would, therefore, affirm the judgment of the Superior Court.

A third case, decided at about the same time as *Beley* and *Harding*, supported the decision that the Korean War was not a "war." *Hawkins v. Metrop. Mutual Assurance Co.*[3] was tried before the Circuit Court of Cook County, Illinois. The insured was drowned while a member of the armed services in Alaska, and the decision was based on determining whether the Korean conflict was a "war" within the provisions of the U.S. Constitution. In its opinion the court stated its belief that if the insurer had meant the word "war" to include an undeclared war, it would have so stated in the policy. Furthermore, the conflict in Korea, declared or undeclared, was not a war between the U.S. and Korea but a war between North and South Korea. Korea was not a member of the United Nations, which had intervened in what might be called a civil war. The United States as a member of the UN contributed its share of forces to carry out an undertaking of the UN. Judgment was rendered for the beneficiary.

2. *Cases in 1952-1956 Holding the Conflict to Be a War*

Within a short time after the first decision in the *Beley* case in the Pennsylvania County Court, another decision was handed down. The Civil Division of the Municipal Court of the District of Columbia in *Gray, Plaintiff v. Southern Aid Life Insurance Co., Defendant*[4] concluded that the Korean situation was the kind of war contemplated in the insurance policy in question. The interpretation announced in *Bennion* was quoted, to the effect that the question to be decided was not whether there had been a political or technical declaration of war in Korea as the word "war" was used in the insurance contract, nor whether there was any formal declaration of war, but rather, what was the purpose and meaning of the words of the contract, and the intent of the parties at the time it was issued. The precedents cited in the opinion were *Bennion, Beley,* (County Court decision) *Darnall v. Day,* and a pre-World War I case, *Stankus v. New York Life Insurance Company.*

The opinion concluded:

> There is no doubt in this court's mind but that this was a "shooting war" in Korea at the time of the death of the insured; that it was and is the kind of war in which the hazard to human life is involved, and this Court concludes that this is the type of war contemplated in the contract of insurance between the parties in this case.

The final decisions in *Beley* and *Harding* in 1953 did not follow the decision in *Gray,* but two cases in other jurisdictions in 1953 were in line with *Gray* (1952).

The opinion in *Weissman v. Metropolitan Life Ins. Co.*[5] was longer and more detailed than the opinion in *Gray.* The primary issue presented to the Court for decision was one of fact—was the Korean conflict a "war" within the meaning of a life insurance policy? This question was answered in the affirmative. The line of reasoning followed in District Court Judge Westover's opinion was summarized in the headnotes:

> 1. *War and National Defense*
> Within strict interpretation of word "war", there can be no war without formal declaration.
>
> 2. *Constitutional Law*
> The existence of war is determined solely by political de-

partments of government, and such determination is conclusively binding on courts in all matters of state or public concern.

3. *Insurance*

If language of insurance policy is reasonably opened to two constructions, that more favorable to insured will be adopted.

4. *Insurance*

Words in insurance policy will be given meaning that common speech imports, unless it is obvious that they are intended to be used in more technical connotation.

5. *Insurance*

In construing insurance policy, court's function and duty is to ascertain and effectuate lawful intention of parties, and in so doing should place itself in position of parties when contract was made and should consider purposes, subject matter, and circumstances under which their minds met.

6. *Insurance*

Insured who was killed in Korea, on August 31, 1951, while in military service of the United States died in military service of the United States when United States was at "war", within double indemnity clause of life policy which excluded death resulting from war.

Portions of the opinion in *Weissman* are quoted:

> The noun "war" is one of those words in the English language which, tho' everyone understands the meaning thereof, few can definitely define. It is probable that when the contract in question was executed there was no discussion between the parties as to the meaning of the term "country at war". At that time the insured was a boy of only fourteen years, and there was possibly no thought in the minds of the parties that the insured within the course of a few years would be inducted into the armed forces and killed while attacking an enemy. Probably the parties who executed the contract understood so well in their own minds the meaning of the term "war" that there was no necessity for further defining it.
>
> • • •
>
> Ever since the adoption of the Constitution there has been controversy as to the meaning of the term "war". The Constitution provides war may be declared only by the Congress; and it is argued there can be no war of which the court may take judicial notice until there has been some act or declaration

creating or recognizing its existence by that department of the government clothed with war-making power. Plaintiff in the case at bar urges that inasmuch as there has been no formal declaration of war, the conflict in Korea is not a war in the strict, legal sense of the word.

[1] Although this nation has been recognized as a peace-loving nation, history indicates there have been very few years of our existence as a nation in which the country has not been engaged in warfare of one kind or another. It is true that on many occasions the conflict was not designated as war by that section of government empowered with the declaration of war, but nevertheless there have been innumerable conflicts in which a great number of troops have been utilized, large expenditures made for munitions, and many casualties suffered. But to those who would hold to the strict interpretation of the term "war" there can be no war without a formal declaration.

[2] This matter has often received the attention of our courts, and the United States Supreme Court has been asked often to pass upon the question of whether the United States was engaged in war, although there had been no formal declaration thereof. One of the earlier decisions handed down by the Supreme Court is that contained in the Prize Cases (The Amy Warwick), 1862, 2 Black. 635, 67 U.S. 635, 17 L.Ed. 459.

• • •

In the case at bar (without admitting it was necessary under the circumstances for Congress to baptize the Korean conflict by giving it the name of "war") it is plain there certainly has been legislative sanction thereof. Because Congress has seen fit to provide money necessary to carry on the conflict, furnish arms, munitions, ships and troops and to proceed in the same manner as if there had been a formal declaration of war, under the authority of the Prize Cases, supra, this court certainly is justified in finding that if such a declaration were necessary, nonetheless, the conflict has received the sanction of Congress.

The federal courts have been consistent in following the rule as laid down in the Prize Cases.

[Quotations from: *Hamilton v. McClaughry,* 136 F. 445; *New York Life Ins. Co. v. Durham,* 166 F.2d 874; *New York Life Ins. Co. v. Bennion,* 158 F.2d 260.]

[4] The Supreme Court has also had occasion to pass upon the question whether, in insurance policies, words which are used by the insurance company shall be interpreted in the

strict, legal sense or considered in their ordinary meaning. In the case at bar plaintiff alleges that since the defendant insurance company used the term "war" in its policy it was employing the term in its strict, legal sense; that is, in the sense that there was no war in the absence of an official declaration thereof. Unfortunately for plaintiff, this contention has been overruled by the Supreme Court of the United States.

In Aschenbrenner v. United States Fidelity & Guaranty Co., 292 U.S. 80, 54 S.Ct. 590, 78 L.Ed. 1137, which went to the Supreme Court on certiorari from the Ninth Circuit, 65 F.2d 976, the court considered the double indemnity provision of an insurance policy.

> [The Circuit Court of Appeals reversed the trial court, and on certiorari the Supreme Court reversed the Circuit Court. The definition of words in an insurance policy was at issue, but the word "war" was not. It was held that, unless it is obvious that the words are intended to be used in their technical connotation, they will be given the meaning that common speech imports.]

[5] Regarding the interpretation of a contract, in New York Life Ins. Co. v. Bennion, supra, the Court said:

> "*** In construing and interpreting the contract between the parties, it is our function and duty to ascertain and effectuate their lawful intention. In so doing, we should place ourselves in the position of the parties when the contract was made, consider the purposes, the subject matter, and the circumstances under which their minds met. [Citing cases.]
>
> * * * * * * * * *
>
> "But we can find nothing in the subject matter, the context, or the purpose of this contract to indicate that the parties intended to use the word war in the technical sense of a formally declared war. The parties did not specify any particular type or kind of war, rather they used the all inclusive term, and we think it only fair to assume that they had in mind any type or kind of war in which the hazard of human life was involved."
>
> [This is followed by a quotation from *Stinson v. New York Life Ins. Co.,* 167 F. 2d 233.]

[6] From the authorities cited above we must come to the conclusion that there may be war (within the meaning of that term employed in an insurance policy) without an official dec-

laration thereof, and that unless it is indicated in the contract that the term "war" is to be used in its strict, legal sense the parties have a right to assume it is to be given its common understanding or meaning.

We doubt very much if there is any question in the minds of the majority of the people of this country that the conflict now raging in Korea can be anything but war. Certainly those who have been called upon to suffer injury and maiming, or to sacrifice their lives, would be unanimous in their opinion that this is war—war in all of its horrible aspects. And the families deprived of the love and companionship of their sons, brothers, husbands and fathers—who meet each day with hope and fear for their boys and men in Korea—and the widows and orphans of the men who died there—certainly they are aware of the stark reality that the Korea conflict is war.

It is the decision of this court that the insured in the case at bar died in the military service of the United States of America at a time when the United States was at war. Judgment is rendered in favor of the defendant.

The second case in 1953 was *Stanbery v. Aetna Life Ins. Co.*,[6] decided in the Law Division of the Superior Court of New Jersey. The opinion opened with consideration of the construction of a contract—specifically, a life insurance policy. The well-established basic rule was defined—to ascertain and determine the intention of the parties as of the time of the making of the contract, as expressed by the language employed when read and considered as a whole. The opinion continued:

[5] In the Beley case the Supreme Court of Pennsylvania, by a four to two vote, held the conflict being waged in Korea is not a war within what may be termed the constitutional or legal sense of that word, and permitted recovery of double indemnity benefit for death of a soldier killed in action in Korea. The opinion of the highest court of a sister state on a similar question is entitled to great respect. However, a reading of the majority and dissenting opinions in that case will demonstrate that the Supreme Court of Pennsylvania gave a legalistic, technical construction of the word "war." Our courts have given the word a realistic interpretation when used in private contracts or documents.

[Ten cases were cited in support.]

The opinion continued with several definitions of "war" (pp. 137-138).

> [7] The word "war" when used in a private contract or document should not be construed on a public or political basis, in a legalistic or technical sense, but should be given its ordinary, usual and realistic meaning, viz., actual hostilities between the armed forces of two or more nations or states de facto or de jure. Schaffer v. Oldak, supra; O'Neill v. Central Leather Co., supra.
>
> The conflict still raging in Korea is a war in the ordinary and usual meaning of the word, and it was such on March 27, 1952, when the insured met his untimely death. See Weissman v. Metropolitan Life Insurance Co., 112 F. Supp. 420 (S.D. Cal. 1953). To hold otherwise and rule the Korean war is not a war seems to me inexplainable and absurd. Borrowing the language of Mr. Justice Bell in his dissenting opinion in the Beley case supra [373 Pa. 231, 95 A.2d 207]:
>
> [Quotation omitted: see *Beley*, above.]
>
> [8] I find and determine that the insured's death resulted from military service in time of war within the intention of the parties as expressed by the language employed in the exclusion clause of the double indemnity provision of the insurance contract, and the judgment is in favor of the defendant Aetna Life Insurance Company, and against the plaintiff Shirley V. Stanbery.

The case of *Western Reserve Life Ins. Co. v. Meadows*[7] was tried and judgment was rendered in 1953 and 1954. The District Court and the Court of Civil Appeals of Texas based their decisions on the definition of "war" as a congressionally declared war. The Supreme Court of the State reversed these judgments, holding that "war" under the life insurance policies in question included the Korean conflict. Rehearing was denied. The U.S. Supreme Court denied certiorari. There were no dissents at any level.

The opinion of the Court of Civil Appeals in the *Meadows* case, based on its decision that the Korean conflict was not a "war," was summarized in the following headnotes:

> 6. *Evidence*
>
> In determining whether conflict in Korea on August 23, 1951,

was "a time of war" within meaning of clause of life policy precluding double indemnity benefits for death occurring while insured was in military service in time of war, court would take judicial knowledge of political history of the world, and would not profess ignorance of momentous events taking place at such time throughout the world.

7. *Evidence*
War and National Defense
The power to declare war is vested exclusively in the legislative department of the federal government, and consequently war, which a court can judicially notice, can never exist without actual concurrence of that body.

• • •

9. *Insurance*
"War", within clause of life policy excluding double indemnity life benefits for death occurring in military service "in time of war", means not merely the employment of force, on however large a scale, but the existence of the legal condition of things in which rights are or may be prosecuted by force.

10. *Insurance*
Death of army officer from airplane crash while traveling as passenger in military aircraft under army orders on August 23, 1951, did not occur in "time of war" within clause of life policy excluding double indemnity benefits for death in military service in "time of war", since, in absence of congressional declaration of war, court could not conclude that condition of Korean controversy was such that state of war existed.

Opinion by Boyd, Justice

• • •

[6] This court must take judicial knowledge of the political history of the world, and we cannot profess ignorance of momentous events taking place on this continent and in other quarters of the globe. World-shaking upheavals, political or military, evidence of which is as near as our newspapers, telephones, radios, and television sets, are things we are bound "to notice and to know." We are not insensible to the sanguinary nature of this conflict and are painfully aware of the 128,000 casualties already sustained by the United States forces in the theater of hostilities, and we know something of the treasure

expended and other sacrifices endured by our people since the invasion of South Korea began. While these observations properly belong to the case, it is nevertheless the duty of a court to ascertain and apply the law to controversies coming before it, uninfluenced by the emotional factors which are inseparable from any contemplation of the existence of a struggle that so profoundly affects us all.

[7] Among the powers granted by the people to the Federal government is the power to declare war, and it was granted to the legislative department exclusively.

[Pages 679-680 contained quotations in support of this position from the following cases:

Bishop v. Jones and Petty
People v. McCleod
Perkins v. Rogers
The Prize Cases
Marks v. U.S.
West v. Palmetto State Life Ins. Co.
Rosenau v. Idaho Mut. Ben. Ass'n.
Savage v. Sun Life Assur. Co.
Pang v. Sun Life Assur. Co.
Opposed to the holdings in these cases, *New York Life Ins. Co. v. Bennion* was quoted.]

We are not called upon to determine whether a "time of war" exists from the moment our country is attacked by the military forces of another nation, and before any declaration of war by Congress, since that question is not before us.

It is significant that in the argument of the steel seizure case, Youngstown Sheet & Tube Co. v. Sawyer, 343 U.S. 579, 72 S.Ct. 863, 897, 96 L.Ed. 1153, the Government did not seek to uphold the President's action under any "war powers."

• • •

The only authorities found from a court of last resort dealing with the question of whether the Korean action is a war are decisions by the Supreme Court of Pennsylvania in the companion cases of Beley v. Pennsylvania Mut. Life Ins. Co., Pa., 95 A.2d 202, 204, and Harding v. Pennsylvania Mut. Life Ins. Co., Pa., 95 A.2d 221, rendered since this case was submitted in this court. The exclusion clauses in both policies considered by that court excepted liability "if said death shall result by reason of *** Military, air or naval service in time of war."

Harding was in military service and was killed September 11, 1950, in a railroad accident en route to a military camp in Indiana. Beley was killed in action in Korea on March 7, 1951, while serving with the United States contingent of the United Nations forces. The court held that neither death occurred while the insured was in the military service "in time of war."

[This was followed by a supporting quotation from *Beley.*]

• • •

[9] War means not merely the employment of force, on however large a scale, but the existence of the legal condition of things in which rights are or may be prosecuted by force. Rosenau v. Idaho Mut. Ben. Ass'n, supra.

If we are to determine from the number of casualties suffered in Korea, or the duration of the conflict, or the financial cost of the operations, that it is a time of war, when should we begin the count?

And if this nation is in a time of war because we have military forces or equipment on foreign waters or foreign soil, we have not seen much time of peace in our history; and if it will be a time of war whenever we are called upon, because of our commitments to the United Nations, to send forces or equipment to foreign waters or foreign soil, it may be that we shall never know another time of peace. And if courts are to decide whether it is a time of war, or a time of peace, by counting the casualties or the cost, by whatever yardstick that to the courts of different states may seem appropriate, we are likely to see the anomalous situation that, by considering the fighting on another continent 8,000 miles away, in some of the states of this union it is a time of peace, and in the others it is a time of war.

[10] War and peace are states of society, at least under our system, and power to declare when we have passed from a state of peace, with its abundant privileges, to a state of war, when the limitations on our privileges arising from that condition may be drastically applied and enforced, ought to be in some central authority of the government, operating alike on all the people in every state, so that all will have the same rights, and the same obligations to the government, at the same time.

We do not believe that this court has the power to declare that a state of war exists between the United States and North Korea, Communist China, Russia, or any other foreign power, and thereby materially affect contractual relations between our citizens, limiting their rights and privileges to those appertaining to a state of society during a time of war, by basing our declaration on some conjectural hypothesis that may be ignored, denied or repudiated in many, if not all, of the other states. We think that this ought to be and is in the exclusive power of the political department of a central government.

If appellant's contention is to be sustained, we must declare that a state of war has existed between this country and some other nation at least since the hostilities in Korea assumed some proportion—just what proportion we do not know—something this court has neither the power nor the inclination to do, and which the war-declaring and war-making department of the government for nearly three years has consistently refused to do. That under the provisions of our Constitution the many courts in the states, without a definite criterion or a uniform standard, and proceeding from different premises and hypotheses, are at liberty to render judgments in conformity with the predilections of the individual judges upon whose decisions the rights to an immense property will be made precariously to depend, is a proposition that does not command the assent of our minds. Courts cannot make the law. If they could and did, we would be cursed by a government of men and not of law, a calamity our people have had the inestimable and happy fortune thus far to escape.

We must believe that the exclusion clause was written and agreed to by the parties in contemplation of the law under which only Congress can declare war, and that it meant the legal state or condition of war. And when the law gives certain words an established meaning, this meaning is less readily controlled by the standard of interpretation otherwise applicable than is the meaning of other words. Rosenau v. Idaho Mut. Ben. Ass'n, supra.

In our view of the case, we think it is unnecessary to determine whether the exclusion clauses are susceptible of more than one interpretation, thus calling for an application of the rule that they must be construed strictly in favor of the insured, although there appears to be authority for such in regard to both clauses. Sun Life Ins. Co. of Canada v. Kiester, supra; Stinson v. New York Life Ins. Co., D.C., 69 F. Supp. 860; Beley v. Pennsylvania Mut. Life Ins. Co., supra.

After a most earnest consideration of the question, and after reviewing all the authorities found by the extensive investigation of counsel, and our own research, we have reached the conclusion that Col. Meadows' death on August 23, 1951, did not occur "in time of war," under the Constitution and laws of the United States and under the terms of the exclusion clause of his insurance policies.

Believing that the able trial court correctly resolved the questions made in the case, the judgment is affirmed.

The Supreme Court of Texas, on appeal, reversed the judgment of the Court of Civil Appeals, holding that, although there was no congressional declaration of war with reference to the Korean conflict, the death of the insured, while in military service, did occur "in time of war" within the double indemnity exclusionary clause. The headnotes of the opinion are quoted, as a summary:

1. *Insurance*
Construction of contracts of insurance is governed by the same rules as other contracts, and terms used in them are to be given their plain, ordinary and generally accepted meaning unless the instrument itself shows them to have been used in a technical or different sense.

2. *War and National Defense*
There may be war or a state of war without a declaration of war by the department of government clothed with the war-making power. U.S.C.A. Const. art. 1, § 8.

3. *Insurance*
"War", within clause of life policy excluding double indemnity benefits for death occurring in military service in time of war, should be considered in practical and realistic sense in which it is commonly used and understood rather than in technical or formal sense.

4. *Insurance*
Although there was never a congressional declaration of war with regard to Korean controversy, the death of army officer from airplane crash while traveling as passenger in military aircraft under army orders on August 23, 1951, did occur in "time of war" within clause of life policy excluding double indemnity benefits for death in military service in "time of war", in absence of anything in insurance contract suggesting that word "war" was used in its technical or legal sense. U.S.C.A. Const. art. 1, § 8.

> 5. *War and National Defense*
>
> The plain, ordinary and generally accepted meaning of the word "war" is war in fact.

The opinion of the court by Justice Smedley opened with a statement of the controlling question—did the accidental death of the insured on August 23, 1951 occur "in time of war"? The decision of the Court of Civil Appeals was reversed, and the court rendered an opinion which reviewed preceding cases, both *pro* and *contra*. The many acts of Congress—*not* including declaration of war—were reviewed, with this conclusion:

> Those Acts were in acknowledgment of the fact of war in which the Nation was engaged. And to use the language of Justice Grier in his opinion in the Prize cases above quoted, if it is necessary to the technical existence of war that it have legislative sanction, the Acts of Congress above referred to gave that sanction.
>
> Decision of this case could well be placed on the ground that if the word "war" used in the policies of insurance was intended to mean "technical war", or "legal war", that is, war declared by Congress, the Acts of Congress prior to the death of the insured should be considered in effect to amount to a declaration of war. We prefer, however, to meet squarely the very question presented, which is whether the word "war" used in the phrase "in time of war" in the policies means war in fact or means war declared by Congress.
>
> [1] It is the settled law in this state that contracts of insurance in their construction are governed by the same rules as other contracts, and that terms used in them are to be given their plain, ordinary and generally accepted meaning unless the instrument itself shows them to have been used in a technical or different sense.
>
> • • •
>
> [2] Undoubtedly there may be war or a state of war without a declaration of war by the department of government clothed with the war-making power. Justice Jackson, in his concurring opinion in the steel mills seizure case said: "Of course, a state of war may in fact exist without a formal declaration." Youngstown Sheet & Tube Co. v. Sawyer, 343 U.S. 579, 72 S.Ct. 863, 873, 96 L.Ed. 1153, 1202-1203, 26 A.L.R. 2d 1378; Edwin

Borchard, discussing under the title "When Did the War Begin", the decision of the United States Circuit Court of Appeals in New York Life Insurance Company v. Bennion, 10 Cir., 158 F. 2d 260, and other decisions, said: "It is common knowledge that war may exist without a declaration thereof." And on the authorities reviewed he expressed this conclusion: "It thus appears that war may be deduced from the circumstances as a fact and may exist independently of a declaration by Congress." 47 Columbia Law Review, pp. 742, 745, 748.

Many definitions of war and many decisions reflect the common understanding of war as war in fact.

[At pp. 557-558 definitions were quoted, drawn from early cases and from *American Jurisprudence* and Black's *Law Dictionary.*]

[3] Decisions involving the question whether and when war has ended are controlled by the same principle, that is, that war exists during the period of actual hostilities and ends with the cessation of those hostilities, even though there has been no treaty of peace or no declaration, proclamation or other official act announcing the termination of the existence of a state of war. In those cases the word "war" is considered as used in the practical and realistic sense in which it is commonly used and understood rather than in a technical or formal sense. See National Life & Accident Ins. Co. v. Leverett, Tex. Civ. App., 215 S.W.2d 939; Lincoln v. Harvey, Tex. Civ. App., 191 S.W.2d 764; New York Life Insurance Co. v. Durham, 10 Cir., 166 F.2d 874; Kaiser v. Hopkins, 6 Cal.2d 537, 58 P.2d 1278; Darnall v. Day, 240 Iowa 665, 37 N.W.2d 277, 280. In the case last cited the court said: "War, in the practical and realistic sense in which it is commonly used, refers to the period of hostilities and not to a technical state of war which may exist after the fighting has ended."

In view of the definitions of "war" above quoted, the decisions mentioned, and the facts about the Korean war set out in the stipulation of the parties and the facts of general knowledge, we are convinced that the accidental death of the insured on August 23, 1951, occurred "in time of war".

• • •

A concurring opinion in Beley v. Pennsylvania Mutual Life Insurance Co. 373 Pa. 231, 95 A.2d 202, 213, by Justice Musmanno, although he joined in the judgment rendered by the majority of four, contains the following significant statements:

"In discussing the principles of law involved in this case, we must assert at once that to deny that the Korean military action is not war in its popularly accepted meaning is to deny the evidence of one's senses. Courts normally take judicial notice of whatever is unquestionably accepted by informed society as fact. A judge does not ask in court for proof that ice forms at the North Pole or that the World Series refers to a contest between baseball teams. Courts know that in Korea, armies are pitted against each other utilizing every device known to modern warfare in the effort and determination to exterminate each other. We know this to be true because every medium of communication extant informs us that it is true. There is not one voice, one printed word, or one picture in the newspapers, radio broadcasts and television images which present themselves before our eyes or appeal to our ears that bespeaks anything to the contrary. In addition, judges have physically seen soldiers who have returned from Korea and have witnessed the evidence of their contact with forces which have inflicted wounds peculiarly the result of gunfire and cannon fire, the trademark of war."

We are unwilling in deciding this case to shut our eyes to what everyone knows, that there has been and was when the insured was killed, actually and in reality a war in Korea in which the United States has been seriously engaged. The Court should not "affect a technical ignorance of the existence" of that war. The same view is expressed in the opinion of the United States Circuit Court of Appeals in New York Life Insurance Company v. Bennion:

• • •

The decision of the Court of Civil Appeals in this cause is supported by several cases cited and discussed in its opinion. Some of those cases may be distinguished from the instant case. Some hold that no war existed under the facts because there was attack but no resistance at the very time; in others the word "war" used in the contract was considered to have been used in a "technical" or "legal" sense.

Beley v. Pennsylvania Mutual Life Insurance Company, 373 Pa. 231, 95 A.2d 202, falls in the class last mentioned. The basis of the opinion holding that the insured, who was killed in battle in Korea on March 7, 1951, was not engaged in military service "in the time of war" is that because a policy of life insurance is highly technical the word "war" in the policy is intended to be used in its technical or legal sense and means a declared war. It is apparent from the opinion, and especially from the quotation which has been set out above from the concurring opinion by Justice Musmanno, that the decision doubtless would have been different if the Court had given the words used in the policy, as they are given in this state, their ordinary and generally understood meaning. The decision in the Beley case was by a majority of four to two, and in our opinion the dissenting opinions are more convincing and are more strongly supported by authority than are the opinions written for the majority.

A very recent opinion by a Superior Court of New Jersey, Stanbery v. Aetna Life Insurance Company, 26 N.J. Super. 498, 98 A.2d 134, 137, holding exactly contrary to the decision of the Pennsylvania court in the Beley case, criticising that decision and declining to follow it, points out that the Pennsylvania court gave a "legalistic, technical construction" of the word "war", whereas the New Jersey courts have given the word a "realistic interpretation when used in private contracts or documents."

In a recent well supported opinion, another trial court, the United States District Court of the Southern District of California, held that there could be no recovery of double indemnity in an action on a life insurance policy which provided for the payment of double indemnity in the event of death of the insured by accidental means, except in the event of the death of the insured while "in the military, naval or air forces of any country at war." The insured, in the military service of the United States, was killed by enemy small arms fire in Korea on August 31, 1951. Weissman v. Metropolitan Life Insurance Co., 112 F.Supp. 420, 421.

The opinion of the Court of Civil Appeals herein in its approval of the Beley case raises the question presented in that case as supporting its decision, how can it be known when a war begins unless there is a formal declaration of war? One of the opinions of the Court in the Beley case contains the following: "Would the appellant insurance company argue that the military action became war when the casualties reached a certain figure, say, 5,000 or 10,000? Would it argue that the action certainly was war when the casualties mounted to 50,000?" 95 A.2d 216. We are not concerned here with the exact time when the Korean war began. It is enough for us to know that war on a large scale had been waged for a long time in Korea and was still being waged when the insured met accidental death.

[4,5] In summary: It is, as has been said, the settled law in this state that, unless a contrary intention is shown by the contract, the terms used in policies of insurance are to be given

> their plain, ordinary and generally accepted meaning. It is clear that nothing in the contract of insurance involved herein suggests that the word "war" is used in its "technical" or "legal" sense. It is clear that the plain, ordinary and generally accepted meaning of the word "war" is war in fact. It is clear that there was war in fact in Korea when the insured was killed and that he was killed "in time of war." It follows that there can be no recovery under the accidental death provisions of the policies.
>
> The judgments of the District Court and Court of Civil Appeals are reversed and judgment is here rendered that respondent take nothing by her suit.

The Supreme Court of the United States denied certiorari in 1954, without an opinion.

Thus, within one year (1953-1954) the U.S. Supreme Court had in effect upheld the Pennsylvania decision in *Beley v. Pennsylvania Mut. Life Ins. Co.*, holding that the Korean conflict *was not* "war" for purposes of determining liability under a life insurance policy, and the Texas decision in *Western Reserve Life Ins. Co. v. Meadows,* holding that the conflict *was* "war" for these purposes. The Supreme Court rendered no opinions in these cases, nor did any justices dissent.

Summarizing the history of decisions bearing on the definition of "war" after the *Beley* and *Harding* decisions and the *Meadows* decision, two lines of decisions are found: (1) all cases in 1954, 1955 and 1956 prior to July 23 of that year followed the principle established in *Meadows*—namely, that the Korean conflict was "war"; (2) on July 23, 1956 the Supreme Court of Colorado rendered judgment in the case of *Pyramid Life Insurance Company v. John William Masch.* The Court held that the Korean conflict was not "war" because Congress did not declare war; and (3) after the *Pyramid* decision, the cases in 1956, 1957, 1959, 1961, and 1965 were based on the pre-*Pyramid* line of cases, following the *Meadows* decision that the Korean conflict was "war" in the context of the several insurance claims.

Fifteen cases based on the Korean conflict were decided after the *Meadows* case in 1953. Six of them were decided by the highest court in the State in which the case arose, and the others were not appealed. None was appealed to the United States Supreme Court. In the following discussion, principal consideration is given to the six cases in the first category.

The U.S. District Court for the Southern District of California, Central Division decided the case of *Podos et al., Plaintiffs v. Equitable Life Assur. Society of U.S., Defendant*[8] in March, 1954. The opinion followed the theory of the earlier cases (*Stanbery, Meadows* and *Weissman*) denying recovery under the policy because, in a realistic sense, the Korean situation was a war, even though undeclared.

The Supreme Court of Iowa, with one justice dissenting, rendered judgment in the case of *Langlas et al. v. Iowa Life Ins. Co.*[9] on April 7, 1954. The headnotes of the opinion summarized the court's opinion:

• • •

4. *Insurance*
The Korean conflict was a "war" within exclusionary clauses in double indemnity provision of life policy and insurer was not liable for double indemnity on death of insured who was killed during active combat duty in Korea. U.S.C.A. Const. art. 1, § 8.

5. *War and National Defense*
The word "war" should be understood in its ordinary sense and the popular connotation of the word is not limited to wars formally declared by Congress to be such. I.C.A. § 427.3, subd. 2, U.S.C.A. Const. art. 1, § 8.

6. *Insurance*
The term "war" as used in exclusionary clauses of double indemnity provision of life policy includes both declared and undeclared wars.

7. *War and National Defense*
"War" in the practical and realistic sense in which it is commonly used, refers to the period of hostilities.

8. *War and National Defense*
The existence of a state of war as determined by political departments of government is binding upon courts only in matters of public concern while as to private contracts the governing principle is the real intent of the parties.

Opinion, Thompson, Justice

• • •

III. The difficulty arises from the fact that the Korean conflict, in which Ervin W. Langlas, Jr., met his death, was commenced, so far as the United States was concerned, without a formal declaration of war.

The United States Constitution, art. 1, § 8, says that only the Congress may declare war; President Truman sent our armed forces into the fighting in Korea without any action from the Congress. The legislative body was at no time thereafter asked to declare that a state of war existed, nor did it ever formally do so. The plaintiffs contend here that the meaning of the term "war" as used in the double indemnity exclusionary clauses is not clear; that it may have referred only to a war formally declared by the Congress; and so the ambiguity which they think exists should be resolved in their favor and against the defendant.

The contention is one which is not without some plausibility, and it has been adopted by a few courts. We think it basically unsound. The purpose of the insurer in inserting the exclusionary clauses in the double indemnity provisions of the two contracts was to protect itself against the greatly added hazards of an actual war. Danger to the life of its assured, and so liability on the part of the company, would be no less because the chief executive, using his power and authority as Commander in Chief of the armed forces of the United States, committed us to a conflict with other nations without the constitutional sanction of a formal declaration by the Congress. This protection was obviously the motive of the insurer, and must have been apparent to the insured. It made no difference to either party to the contract whether the Congress acted; the executive committed us to a real and bitter war. Nor was this in any sense unusual. Phillipson, in his International Law and The Great War, page 53, points out that of 118 recognized wars occurring between 1700 and 1872, in only ten was there a formal declaration preceding the commencement of hostilities.

[4] In fact, it has long been recognized that the executive may, in many ways, embroil his country in war, so that the legislature has no opportunity to prevent it and no choice but to accept it as an accomplished fact. Or the war may result from a sudden attack by a hostile nation, requiring immediate retaliation before the Congress has any opportunity to act. With the present possibilities of guided missiles and rapid flight with

loads of highly destructive bombs, he is naive indeed who will say we must wait until a formal declaration is promulgated before we are at war. Adopting the term "war" as it is now commonly understood, and looking to the evident purpose the language in the exclusionary clauses was intended to serve, we must hold the Korean conflict was a "war" within the meaning of the contracts. There is no room for application of the rule contended for by plaintiffs.

The unreality of adopting an interpretation which would hold the Korean struggle not to be a war within any reasonable meaning is pointed up by the fact that as of March 28, 1952 (three days after the insured met his death in the fighting), total United States casualties were 106,956, with 16,739 killed and 77,651 wounded and 9,916 missing in action. Of all wars in which this country has been engaged, only the two World Wars and Civil War exceeded the Korean struggle in cost in casualties and money.

[5] The plaintiffs urge that the insurer could have made the language clearer and more definite by specifying that an "undeclared" war as well as a declared one was meant. Since we think the word "war" is to be understood in its ordinary sense, and further that the popular connotation of the word is by no means limited to wars formally declared by the Congress to be such, we are unable to agree. Many conflicts have been referred to as "wars" when there was no formal declaration.

[Citations to earlier cases included definitions of "war."]

[6] All of the foregoing authorities recognize that war is a fact, not dependent upon the formal declaration of Congress. More than that, they demonstrate the ordinary and common understanding of the term. If armed forces of two nations are in conflict, the ordinary observer knows they are at war; and he is not likely to draw fine distinctions. In common understanding war is war, whether declared or undeclared. Under the general definition of war, the term used in the double indemnity clauses included both declared and undeclared wars, and there was no need for a more particular designation. The whole is greater than any of its parts, and includes all of them.

[7] We have ourselves recognized this principle. In Darnall v. Day 240 Iowa 665, 37 N.W.2d 277, we were concerned with an agreement on the part of a building owner to make certain improvements within one year after the close of World War II. More than one year after the close of actual hostilities, but

before any official pronouncement of the end of the war, the remodeling had not been done by the landlord, and litigation developed. We held the war had ended within the meaning of the agreement; that it was the close of the fighting which was intended.

[*Durham, Stinson* and *Bennion* were cited in support.]

[8] We also pointed out in the Darnall case that the existence of a state of war as determined by the political departments of government is binding upon the courts only in matters of public concern; while as to private contracts the governing principle is the real intent of the parties. New York Life Insurance Company v. Durham, supra, and Stinson v. New York Life Insurance Company, supra, were cited and followed on this point.

IV. A good case might be made for the contention that although the Congress did not officially declare a state of war to exist, it did for all practical purposes and in substantial effect recognize and ratify its existence.

[The different acts of Congress supporting this statement were listed.]

There can be no doubt the Congress itself recognized the struggle as a "war." Since we hold there is no ambiguity in the language of the contracts, and the words must be taken in their common meaning, there is no occasion to go further into the question of ratification; but a strong argument might be made for such a holding.

V. The case has been argued here by the plaintiffs on the theory that the contracts must be interpreted to mean there is no war unless the Congress of the United States has officially declared it to exist. The possibility of loss of life by the insured in a war in which other nations are involved has not been considered. Yet if we are correct in holding the real purpose of the exclusionary clauses was to protect against the abnormal and excessive risk incurred in war, declared or undeclared, it must appear liability is excluded if the insured engages in any war, even one in which the United States might not be involved. Many American fighting men, in both World Wars, enlisted in the Canadian service before this country was involved. In Korea, the Republic of Korea and many allies, in addition to the armed forces of the United States, members of the United Nations, were fighting the North Korean and Chinese Communist forces. Even if it were possible to say we were never in war in Korea because it was not declared, there was surely a war between many other nations there. In Stankus v. New York Life Insurance Company, supra, the insured lost his life through naval action while serving upon a United States destroyer on convoy duty in the Atlantic, before we entered World War II. The Massachusetts Supreme Court said there was at least a war going on between Great Britain and Germany and the insured lost his life as an incident thereto.

• • •

VII. The identical question here involved has been considered by several courts since the outbreak of the fighting in Korea. Of these, only two are courts of last resort, and they have taken opposite positions. The plaintiffs cite and rely much upon Beley v. Pennsylvania Mutual Life Insurance Company and Harding v. Pennsylvania Mutual Life Insurance Company. They were decided by the Supreme Court of Pennsylvania on February 14, 1953, and the opinions are found in 373 Pa. 231, 95 A.2d 202, and 373 Pa. 270, 95 A.2d 221, respectively. The majority concurring opinions in the Beley case hold to the technical viewpoint, construing the intent of the parties to have contemplated a war declared by the Congress by virtue of its constitutional authority. The cases were decided by a four to two vote of the court, and we agree with the logic and authorities of the dissenting opinions.

The Supreme Court of Texas had the Pennsylvania cases before it when it handed down its opinion on October 7, 1953, in Western Reserve Life Insurance Company v. Meadows, Tex., 261 S.W.2d 554. The Texas court took what we think the sounder position, holding the Korean conflict to be a "war" within the intent of the insurance contract. Our agreement with the reasoning of the Texas court has already been indicated, and we have cited and followed many of the same authorities.

Other courts not of final authority have had the question before them.

[*Weissman, Stanbery* and *Bennion* were cited, with quotations. Reference was made to cases contra–*Bennion, Palmetto, Rosenau* and *Savage.*]

So far as these cases are in point, we do not agree with this reasoning and do not find them persuasive.

Our own case of Darnall v. Day, supra, has been widely cited and approved. The reasoning of this case still satisfies us, and we think it controlling, supported as it is by the many authorities above referred to.

VIII. A special concurring opinion in Beley v. Pennsylvania Mutual Life Insurance Company, supra, poses some questions which have been adopted by the plaintiffs herein, and which should be given attention. It is asked, when did the Korean conflict become a war? How many casualties, 5,000 or 10,000, or more, must have been sustained before it would be a war? Who is to determine at what point in time or casualties an undeclared struggle becomes a "war" within the meaning of the terms of insurance contracts excluding liability for deaths as the result of "war"? The method of proving his point used by the learned Pennsylvania justice is not an unusual one; but we do not agree with plaintiffs' counsel that the questions are unanswerable. At least they are not so in the sense that they have any important bearing on the case before us. We are not, in fact, concerned with the answers to the questions posed. What we must know is whether the Korean conflict, as it stood on March 25, 1952, when Ervin W. Langlas, Jr. met his death on the battlefield was a "war" within the commonly understood meaning of the word. If it was such, as we have concluded, we need not go into fine distinctions as to when it became so, nor how many casualties or how much expenditure of blood and treasure made it so. In the words of Justice Smith, in City of Des Moines v. City of West Des Moines, 239 Iowa 1, 14, 30 N.W.2d 500, 507: "There will be time enough to bid the Devil 'good morrow' when we meet him."

We conclude the terms of the double indemnity clauses were clear and unambiguous, and are effective to prevent recovery by the plaintiffs. The case is reversed, with directions to enter judgment for the defendant on each count. Reversed, with directions.

BLISS, C. J., and MULRONEY, SMITH, GARFIELD, WENNERSTRUM, HAYS, and LARSON, JJ., concur.

OLIVER, J., dissents.

In June, 1954 the U.S. District Court for the Massachusetts District announced its decision in the case of *Gagliormella et al. v. Metropolitan Life Ins. Co.*[10] The issue in the case was whether a U.S. marine, killed in military action in Korea on October 31, 1952, was killed "as a result of an act of war," within the meaning of a life policy providing for additional death benefits for violent death if such death had not occurred as a result of an act of "war." The court held that the Korean conflict was "war." The Massachusetts courts had not squarely addressed themselves to this issue, although in the *Stankus* case[11] in 1942 war had been defined to include every situation that ordinary people would commonly regard as war. Full details were matters of common knowledge and needed no restatement. The court's conclusion was supported by *Weissman, Meadows, Stanbery* and *Langlas.* Perhaps the contrary decision in *Beley* could have been distinguished because of the precise terms and contrasting provisions of the policy therein considered but, if not, the court was constrained to believe that the Massachusetts State court would not accept its holding as a governing precedent.

Carius v. New York Life Ins. Co.[12] was decided by the U.S. District Court, S.D. Illinois, N.D. in December, 1954. The court held that Major Carius's death, suffered in actual combat in North Korea, resulted from war or an act incident to war "in the plain, ordinary and popular sense of the words" used in the double indemnity coverage clause contained in the policy sued upon.

The case of *Helen Gudewicz v. John Hancock Mutual Life Insurance Company*[13] was considered by the highest court in Massachusetts—the Supreme Judicial Council—with a decision on December 1, 1954. The Superior Court, Bristol County, had reported the case, which was presented on a case stated, without making any decision.

The two headnotes summarized the decision of the Supreme Judicial Council:

> 1. *Insurance*
>
> Under a life policy excluding additional benefits if death of insured occurred while in military service during time of war, the word "war" includes everything that ordinary people regard as war, and includes the conflict between armed forces of different nations under authority of their respective governments.
>
> 2. *Insurance*
>
> Under life policy providing additional benefits for death caused by bodily injury sustained solely by external, violent and

accidental means but denying additional benefits if death occurred while insured was in naval service in time of "war", declared or undeclared, insurer was not liable for death of insured in automobile accident on furlough while in naval service during the war in Korea, although his death was not a result of his service.

The opinion stated by Justice Lummus is quoted in part, below:

> The only question is, whether the death of the insured occurred "while the insured is in military, naval or air service in time of war, whether such war be declared or undeclared." The Superior Court reported the case, which was presented on a case stated, without making any decision.
>
> [1] The fighting in Korea was not preceded or accompanied by any declaration of war. But that has been true of many wars. In a policy of insurance, the word "war" includes everything that ordinary people regard as war, and clearly includes a conflict between the armed forces of different nations under the authority of their respective government. [*Stankus* and *Langlas* were cited.]
>
> [2] Under the policy, the defendant escapes liability if the insured was in naval service when he died, although his death was not the result of his service.
>
> • • •
>
> Judgment for the defendant.

In April, 1955 the St. Louis Court of Appeals in Missouri decided the case of *Robert J. Lynch (Plaintiff), Appellant, v. The National Life and Accident Insurance Company, a Corporation (Defendant), Respondent.*[14] Previously, the Magistrate's Court had given judgment for the Company, and the Circuit Court of the City of St. Louis had upheld the decision. The Court of Appeals affirmed this judgment, holding that the Korean conflict was a "war" within the war clause of the insurance policy, although there had been no declaration by Congress. One interesting portion of the opinion (pp. 34-38) contained definitions of "war" taken from 17 different sources, most of them opinions in cases.

The Supreme Court of Washington, Department 2, announced its decision in May, 1955 in the case of *Martin Christensen, Appellant, v. Sterling Insurance Company, Respondent*[15], affirming the judgment of the Superior Court of Pierce County, and declaring that the Korean conflict was a "war."

The headnotes constitute a summary of the opinion:

1. *Evidence*
In purely private matters courts may take judicial notice that a war exists.

2. *Contracts*
Parties to a contract may use the term "war" in other than its strict constitutional sense.

3. *Insurance*
In construing life insurance contracts court seeks to determine intent of the parties and general rules governing construction of contracts must be applied.

4. *Insurance*
The court will give language used in insurance contract the ordinary and popular meaning, unless a different meaning is apparent from a reading of the whole contract.

5. *War and National Defense*
A conflict in which military forces of two or more governments meet in armed conflict over an extended period of time is a "war" in the popular sense of the word.

6. *Insurance*
Where the apparent objective of a war service clause of life policy was to define a risk and exclude it from coverage under the policy, the parties to the insurance contract meant "war" in the popular sense rather than the strict sense which requires a formal declaration of war by Congress.

7. *Insurance*
Where insured was killed in Alaska while in the United States military service during time of Korean conflict, and policy on his life excluded payment, except for refund of premiums or reserve value, for death from any cause while in military service of any "country at war" the United States was a country at war within policy.

Quoting from the opinion by Justice Weaver, in which four justices concurred:

> Was the United States a "country at war" on May 11, 1952 (during the Korean conflict), within the meaning of the terms of a life insurance policy?
>
> The answer is to be found within the scope and meaning of the word "war." Is it to be construed in its legal or technical sense, or is it to be given its ordinary meaning as used in common speech?
>
> Such construction becomes important in four distinct situations which concern an insured in military service:
>
> First: Where death occurs prior to the formal declaration of war, as, for example, during the attack on Pearl Harbor, December 7, 1941; the official declaration of war by Congress being made the following day.
>
> Second: Where death occurs while the armed forces of the country are engaged in combat in which a formal declaration of war was never made.
>
> Third: Where death occurs after the cessation of hostilities in a formally declared war, but before the war is officially ended.
>
> Fourth: Where death occurs after the cessation of hostilities in an armed conflict in which a formal declaration of war never was made.
>
> We are concerned, in this case, with a factual situation arising under the second category.
>
> The insured died as a result of an automobile accident in Alaska, on May 11, 1952, while he was serving in the military service of the United States.
>
> The life insurance policy, on which this action by the beneficiary is based, contains a "war service" clause that provides:
>
> "If the Insured shall die from any cause while in Military, Naval or Air Service of *any country at war* *** Company shall be liable only for a refund of the premiums paid, or the reserve *** whichever is greater. ***" (Italics ours.)

The plaintiff Christensen relied on the decisions in earlier cases—*Beley, Harding, Rosenau, Palmetto* and *Savage*—to the effect that a court cannot take judicial notice of the existence of a war until a formal declaration has been made by the proper department of the Federal government. Other courts had held that, in private matters, unaffected by a public interest, the courts were free to take judicial notice of the existence of a war although no formal declaration of war had been made by the Federal government. In such cases, the courts had construed "war" in its ordinary, popular sense, holding that the Korean conflict was a war within the meaning of the terms of the policy. Supporting cases were cited—*Meadows, Langlas, Stanbery, Weissman* and *Gagliormella.*

The opinion continued:

> We cannot subscribe to the reasoning of the Beley case, supra, and those decisions which have followed it. To our mind, it overlooks four considerations which are controlling.
>
> [1] First: in matters which are purely private courts may take judicial notice that a war exists.
>
> Second: the word "war", as it is generally understood, involves armed conflict between the military forces of two or more nations. Its existence does not depend upon a declaration by Congress. "In common understanding, war is war, whether declared or undeclared." Langlas v. Iowa Life Ins. Co., supra.
>
> Third: it ignores the well-known purpose of insurers.
>
> Fourth: the legalistic determination of the question ignores the *modus operandi* of the United Nations. As one legal writer observed:
>
> "* * * if the Charter of the United Nations is strictly applied, war of the declared or constitutional type may be for historians." Cecil J. Olmstead, 1953 Annual Survey of American Law, page 12.
>
> [2] This court has recognized the right of parties to a contract to use the term "war" in other than its strict, constitutional sense. Hoover v. Sandifur, 1946, 25 Wash. 2d 791, 171 P.2d 1009, 168 A.L.R. 170.
>
> [3,4] When construing the terms of a policy of insurance, the court seeks to determine the intent of the parties, and the general rules governing the construction of contracts must be

applied. The people to whom policies of insurance are issued consider and understand the terms in their popular and ordinary meaning, Kane v. Order of United Com. Travelers, 1940, 3 Wash. 2d 355, 360, 100 P.2d 1036, and the court will give the language used such a construction.

"*** unless it is apparent from a reading of the whole instrument that a different or special meaning was intended or is necessary in order to avoid an absurd or unreasonable result." Richards v. Metropolitan Life Ins. Co., 1935, 184 Wash. 595, 601, 55 P.2d 1067, 1069.

[5] When, as in Korea, the military forces of two or more nations, under the direction of their governments, meet in armed combat over an extended period of time and in numerous engagements, such activity is ordinarily called "war." It is war in the ordinary, popular sense of the word.

A reading of the whole instrument does not disclose that a different or special meaning was intended by the words "country at war."

[6,7] The purpose of a war service clause is to define a risk and exclude it from the general coverage of the policy. If "war" is given its ordinary, popular meaning, liability is determined by actual combat, a factor which naturally affects the risk; if given its strict, constitutional meaning, liability is determined by a formal declaration which, unless coupled with actual combat, does not increase or decrease the risk. In the light of the apparent object of the clause, we conclude that the parties did not intend to have the language used, construed in its strict, technical sense.

The United States was a "country at war," within the meaning of the terms of the policy.

The judgment dismissing the action is affirmed.

The Municipal Court of New York, Borough of Manhattan, Second District announced in May, 1956 its decision in the case of *Samuel N. Wilkinson and Mary A. Wilkinson, Plaintiffs, v. The Equitable Life Assurance Society of the United States, Defendant.*[16]

So far as could be ascertained by the court, the courts of New York State had not had occasion to consider whether the fighting in Korea was to be considered "war, whether declared or undeclared" within the exclusionary provision contained in this life insurance policy. The question, however, had been presented in several other jurisdictions, both state and federal. The *Podos* case was cited as authority. Accepting the rule that the "plain, ordinary and generally accepted meaning of the word 'war' is war in fact," the court held that there could be no doubt that the United States was engaged in a war in Korea as an actual fact, even though there had been no declaration by Congress. The statement in the opinion concerning the *Beley* and *Harding* cases is quoted:

> In those cases, the Court held that since there had been no formal declaration of war, the Korean fight was not to be considered war. The exclusionary language, however, was not nearly as specific or precise as in this case. It merely excluded death resulting from military service in time of war, without the addition of the words "whether declared or undeclared". The majority opinion in the Beley case suggests that there would have been a holding to the contrary if the words "declared or undeclared" had been added.

3. *Decision of July 23, 1956 Holding the Conflict Not a War*

Although the series of cases since *Meadows* had held that the Korean conflict was "war," the Supreme Court of Colorado did not follow these precedents in deciding *Pyramid Life Insurance Company, a Kansas Corporation, Plaintiff in Error, v. John William Masch, Defendant in Error,*[17] in July 1956. The relevant headnotes are quoted:

> 3. *Constitutional Law*
> The existence or nonexistence of a state of war is a political, not a judicial, question and it is only when a formal declaration of war has been made by Congress that judicial cognizance may be taken thereof and once so declared by the political department, it becomes binding upon the parties, otherwise not.
>
> 4. *Evidence*
> The courts could not take judicial notice that the engagement of United States troops in Korea constituted "war" notwithstanding that war was never declared by Congress.

5. *Insurance*

Where life policy was prepared by the defendant it must stand by the words employed in the policy.

6. *Insurance*

Any doubt concerning the meaning of a word or clause in a life policy should be resolved in favor of insured.

7. *Insurance*

Death of insured while in military service of the United States Army in the Korean conflict did not occur "in time of war" within exception of the policy limiting the liability of insurer to the premiums paid on the policy in view that "war" was never declared by Congress with respect to the action in Korea.

The Supreme Court of Colorado upheld the judgment of the District Court of Las Animas County.

Quoting relevant portions of the opinion:

[3,4] We are asked to take judicial notice that the engagements of United States troops in Korea constituted "War"; this, in spite of the fact, as counsel for defendant admit, that "war" was never declared by Congress, the only authority competent to declare it, with respect to the action in Korea. The existence or nonexistence of a state of war is a political, not a judicial, question and it is only when a formal declaration of war had been made by the Congress that judicial cognizance may be taken thereof. Once so declared by the political department, it becomes binding upon the courts, otherwise not.

[Cases cited were *Rosenau, Beley* and *Palmetto*.]

[5] The contract in the instant case was prepared by the officers and agents of the defendant and as insurer it must stand by the words employed in the policy. If the words "in time of war" were to include every type of hostility that might occur between the armed forces of different nations, without an open declaration of war, an insurer could not possibly know its liability under such a contract until some court decided whether or not the hostilities referred to constituted a "war".

[6,7] Any doubt concerning the meaning of a word or clause in a life insurance policy should be resolved in favor of the insured. Had the defendant desired to cover the contingency here involved it would have been a simple matter to include

> proper words to indicate that "war" meant "hostilities", whether or not declared by Congress to be a state of war.
>
> We perceive no error in the ruling of the trial court, hence the judgment is affirmed.

4. *Cases in 1956-1965 Holding the Conflict to Be a War*

In July, 1956 the Superior Court of Connecticut in Fairfield County announced its decision in the case of *Anna Zaccardo v. John Hancock Mutual Life Insurance Co.*[18] Basing its decision on the judgments in *Gudewicz, Stankus* and *Langlas,* no mention was made of *Pyramid, Beley* or other cases holding that the Korean conflict was *not* "war." The court held that whether "declared or undeclared" the conflict was war in fact. Although Congress had not formally declared war, it had by implication recognized the existence of such a state by providing benefits for those who served in our forces after June 15, 1950 comparable to those provided for veterans of both world wars. The Connecticut legislature had taken similar action.

The Supreme Court of Pennsylvania, which had rendered the important decisions in *Beley* and *Harding* in 1953, was faced with a second important situation in 1957. Their decision on March 25 of that year, in the case of *Francis R. Thomas, Sr., Appellant, v. Metropolitan Life Insurance Company,*[19] constituted an apparent reversal of the two earlier decisions, although the court in the *Thomas* decision went to great lengths to establish a difference between the wording of the policies in the two cases. To what extent a change in membership of the Pennsylvania Supreme Court affected the *Thomas* decision cannot be established. Two members of the 1953 court had been replaced by two new members by 1957, and one member who did not participate in 1953 did vote in 1957. Thus, three votes are eliminated in making the comparison. One justice who voted with the majority in 1953 maintained his own view by dissenting in 1957. Two justices who dissented in 1953 were consistent in voting with the majority in 1957. One justice changed his position, voting with the majority in both cases. Thus the four-to-two (with one justice not voting) decision in 1953 became a six-to-one decision in 1957.

A majority of the court in the *Thomas* decision joined in a *per curiam* opinion, and Justice Musmanno wrote a dissenting opinion. The headnotes are quoted as a summary:

> 1. *War and National Defense*
> The generally accepted meaning of the word "war" is an armed conflict between two nations; in its constitutional and legal sense it means a formally declared war by the authorities authorized to declare war, unless it has been so characterized to impart an entirely different meaning.
>
> 2. *Insurance*
> If phrase used in insurance policy was ambiguous, it would have to be interpreted most strongly against insurer who drew the contract.
>
> 3. *Insurance*
> Where double indemnity provision of life policy specified payment of additional benefits for death through accidental means except where death was the result of "act of war", insured who was killed in Korean conflict and who was awarded the Navy Cross posthumously met death as a result of "act of war", and insurer was not liable for double indemnity benefit, notwithstanding that war was not formally declared and that armed units of United Nations members took part in the conflict. 10 U.S.C.A. § 6242.
>
> 4. *Insurance*
> An "act of war" within life policy providing benefit for accidental death not occurring as result of act of war is an attack by the armed forces of one nation against the armed forces or civilians of another nation; it is the invasion of territory of one nation by armed forces of another; the hostile attack may occur without war being declared formally or informally, and without either country recognizing existence of state of war.

The court of Common Pleas of Allegheny County had entered judgment for the insurance company (No. 3212, April term, 1955) and the beneficiary appealed; the Supreme Court of Pennsylvania affirmed this judgment (March 25, 1957) and denied rehearing (April 17, 1957).

The *per curiam* opinion of the majority of the Supreme Court consisted entirely of quotation from the opinion of Judge Loran S. Lewis in the decision by the Court of Common Pleas.

The insured was killed in combat in Korea, and the company paid the face amount of the policy but refused to pay double indemnity because they contended that the insured was killed "as a result of an *act of war*."

> "The plaintiff contends the Insured was not killed by an 'act of war' because no war existed between the United States and any other nation. While the plaintiff's counsel admits that the struggle in Korea involved armed conflict between a group of nations, yet he argues it could not be considered a war, because the United States had not formally declared war on the North Koreans or the Chinese Communists.
>
> "In support of this argument, the plaintiff cites the recent case of Beley v. Pennsylvania Mutual Life Insurance Company, a Corporation, 373 Pa. 231 [95 A.2d 202, 36 A.L.R.2d 996].
>
> [1] "We must first determine then what we mean by the term 'war'.
>
> "While the generally accepted meaning of the word 'war' is an armed conflict between two nations, according to the various opinions handed down by the many courts throughout the land, the legal interpretation of the word 'war' is not as simple as it would seem. Beginning with the earliest cases, there has been a marked conflict, not only between the different courts, but between judges of the same court, as to the legal interpretation of the word 'war'.
>
> "In our own state of Pennsylvania, in the Beley case, supra, four justices interpreted 'war' to mean one thing and two others gave it an entirely different meaning.
>
> "This difference of opinion is largely due to the fact that the courts from the earliest days recognized that wars fall into one of two classifications. They are either declared or undeclared."

The opinion next reviewed cases preceding *Beley*, with this conclusion:

> "It will be noted that the above engagements of force against other nations without a formal declaration of war by Congress

have been referred to by the term War by our historians and our courts.

"It becomes very clear then that hostilities between nations can become war whether solemnly declared or not. War of the perfect kind, solemnly declared, is called declared war. War of the imperfect kind that has not been baptized with a name by Congress is known as undeclared war."

The opinion continued:

"The majority opinion in the case of Beley v. Pennsylvania Mutual Life Insurance Company, a Corporation, supra, on which the plaintiff relies, while contending that 'war' as used in the policy means a formally declared war by Congress, recognized the fact, however, that there are two kinds of wars, declared and undeclared.

"In permitting a recovery on the policy in the Beley case, for the death of the insured in Korea while a member of the armed forces, for the face amount of the policy and double indemnity, under a policy which contained a clause limiting recovery to the return of premiums if the insured engaged in military or naval service in the time of war, the courts said [373 Pa. 231, 95 A.2d 205]:

" 'The action being waged in Korea is not a "war" within what may be termed the "constitutional" or "legal" sense of that term.'

"It is apparent from reading the opinion of the majority that the court recognized the fact that there were two kinds of war but in interpreting the language contained in the insurance policy they decided that it must be given its constitutional or legal meaning or otherwise the court would be utterly at sea whenever a question arose as to whether certain expeditions in which the United States forces were engaged constituted a war.

"The court concluded in the Beley case that if the insurance company intended that 'war' should have a broader connotation than its constitutional or legal intendment it merely had to add to the term 'war' in the contract, 'declared or undeclared'.

"Since the Beley case, supra, and its companion case, Harding v. Pennsylvania Mutual Life Insurance Company, 373 Pa. 270 [95 A.2d 221], Id., 171 Pa. Super. 236 [90 A.2d 589], were decided, similar cases in other jurisdictions have been decided, which held that the conflict in Korea was a war within the meaning of an insurance clause excluding death from war. [Cases cited were *Meadows, Langlas, Gudewicz, Gagliormella, Carius* and *Christensen.*]

"These cases all have adopted the view that war existed in Korea because the armies of nations were in armed conflict and therefore war existed.

"The Supreme Court of Pennsylvania, while admitting that war in the generally accepted sense did exist, was more concerned with the proper interpretation of the war exclusion clause in the insurance contract, which was the real issue in the Beley case.

"Finding that the term 'war' for over one hundred fifty years has been classified as declared or undeclared by the various courts throughout the nation, they concluded that the term 'war' was ambiguous and should be most strongly construed against the insurance company, whose lawyers drafted the contract.

"In so doing, they concluded that war must be construed in its constitutional and legal sense, which means a formally declared war by Congress.

"The learned Judge Dithrich of the Superior Court, who wrote the opinion in the Harding case, supra, which was affirmed by the Supreme Court of Pennsylvania, had this to say [171 Pa. Super. 236, 90 A.2d 597].

" 'Since "war" is a word which has been held to import various meanings, it is incumbent upon the insurer to make clear that it applies to undeclared war, as well as to declared war, for even if the action in Korea should be held to be war, it is at most an undeclared war.'

"It is our opinion that the reasoning of the Supreme Court in the Beley and Harding cases, supra, was not only logical and clear, but the result just.

"Furthermore, we are bound by the decision and must accept the term 'war' in its constitutional and legal sense to mean a formally declared war by the authorities authorized to declare war, unless it has been so characterized to impart an entirely different meaning.

"In the instant case, however, the plaintiff's right of recovery rises or falls on the legal interpretation of the phrase, *'act of war*'. If the Insured came to his death as a result of an 'act of war', plaintiff beneficiary cannot recover in the instant case.

[2] "If the term 'act of war' is also an ambiguous term and has two or more meanings, it would have to be interpreted most strongly against the defendant insurance company, who drew the contract. Ebbert v. Philadelphia Electric Co., 330 Pa. 257 [198 A. 323].

[3] "The plaintiff contends the phrase, 'act of war', as referred to in the policy, refers to an act pertaining to a formally declared war, and as the Supreme Court in the Beley case has decided the Korean conflict was not a war, not being formally declared, the clause excluding recovery by reason of death caused by an act of war, does not prevent recovery in this case.

[4] "It is our opinion, however, that the term 'act of war' is not an ambiguous term. It has been used many times in connection with the description of an attack by the armed forces of one nation against the armed forces of another. It has been used in connection with the attack by the armed forces of one nation against the civilians of another; and it has been used in connection within the invasion of the territory of one nation by the armed forces of another.

"These hostile attacks may occur without war being declared formally or informally, and without either country recognizing the existence of a state of war."

This point was expanded by citing earlier decisions and scholarly definitions, including the following:

"Justice Musmanno in his very excellent and scholarly opinion in the Beley case, supra, made a clear distinction between 'a state of war' and 'an act of war', when he said [373 Pa. 231, 95 A.2d 216]:

" 'There can be acts of war without there being a state of war. Beley was killed by an act of war but not in a state of war.'

"If it is true that Beley was killed by an act of war, then it would seem that Francis R. Thomas, Jr. the Insured in the instant case, also met his death by an act of war. Both met their death in Korea by enemy action.

"The plaintiff's counsel agrees that an act of war relates to an act of aggression or hostility committed by one nation against another, such as the bombing of Pearl Harbor, or the sinking of the Lusitania, or perhaps, an act of serious sabotage by the agents of one government against another such as might induce a condition of war or a state of war. He argues, however, that the conflict in Korea cannot in any sense be an attack upon the sovereignty or territory of the United States because the military action which took place there was under the guise and authority of the United Nations members in which the various components sent armed units."

• • •

"The only case we can find involving similar language to the language used in the insurance policy in the instant case is the case of Gagliormella v. Metropolitan Life Insurance Company, 122 F.Supp. 246.

"In that case, the insured was killed in Korea on October 21, 1952, which was four days prior to the death of the Insured in the case at bar.

"In determining that the insured was killed by an act of war and that the beneficiary was not entitled to double indemnity under the accidental coverage, the court stated:

"'It is even clearer that (to use the language of policy 17 989 790A) the insured's death occurred as a result of an act of war. Under this second policy it would not even be necessary to find that the United States was at war; it would be quite enough to find that either North Korea or South Korea was at war. See Stankus v. N.Y. Life Ins. Co. [312 Mass. 366, 44 N.E.2d 687]. And those two powers were surely in a belligerent status.'

"Whether the Insured in the instant case came to his death while engaged in a conflict in which at least two of the belligerents were actually at war, or whether he came to his death while fighting as a soldier in the United States Army in an undeclared war, seems of no moment, because an act of war has never been specifically identified with either a declared or undeclared war.

"As we have seen, an act of war can be committed without the act ever culminating in a war either declared or undeclared.

"A whole continuing series of acts of war may be committed by belligerents without either belligerent formally or informally recognizing the existence of a state of war.

"Even the warlike act of an individual soldier under orders of a commanding officer and sanctioned by a recognized government may be classified as an act of war.

"If we were to consider an act of war to be a warlike act committed in carrying out a formally declared war, as advocated by the plaintiff, we would be casting aside the generally accepted definition of an act of war in favor of an entirely new concept of the term.

"If the term 'act of war' is ambiguous and can have two meanings, just as the word 'war' has, then it would be incumbent on us to construe it most strongly against the insurance company, who drew the contract of insurance, and hold an act of war only has reference to formally declared war.

"Prior court decisions buttressed by historical fact are all exceedingly clear, however, as to the meaning of the term 'acts of war', which we have seen has never been specifically associated with a formally declared war.

"According to the agreed statement of facts at the time of the Insured's death, he was a member of Company 'C', First Battalion, 7th Marines, First Marine Division, engaged in combat with the military forces of North Korea and the Chinese People's Army.

"From the citation accompanying the awarding of the Navy Cross posthumously given the Insured, his heroism in the particular engagement with the enemy must have been one of the most courageous exploits of the war.

"His deeds will be forever enshrined with the records of the noblest and most courageous of the United States Marines.

"Can anyone seriously argue that the Insured did not come to his death by an act of war while fighting for his country?

"His own government recognized the fact that he was killed by an act of war in awarding him the Navy Cross.

"This citation is only awarded to a person 'who *** distinguishes himself by extraordinary heroism in connection with military operations against an armed enemy.' (56 Statute 743 [34] U.S.C.A. Section 356*).

"We are, therefore, of the opinion that the Insured came to his death through an act of war."

Judgment affirmed.

MUSMANNO, Justice.

---

*Now 10 U.S.C.A. § 6242.

I find myself somewhat trammeled in preparing my dissent in this case because the Majority of the Court did not write an opinion of its own, but accepted almost wholly the opinion of Judge Loran Lewis of the Court of Common Pleas of Allegheny County. Judge Lewis is a jurist of distinguished qualifications and, if I may allow myself a personal reference, he is a close and respected friend. I agree with my colleagues here that Judge Lewis wrote an able opinion. I will go further and say that he wrote a brilliant opinion. The only difficulty about it, as I see it, is that he deviated from a decision rendered by this Court quite recently on the very same subject.[1*]

In writing this Dissenting Opinion, however, I shall address myself to my colleagues and not to Judge Lewis. The members of the Court below did their duty as they saw it. The writer of their opinion was exhausting in his research, profound in his analysis, and his expression has imprinted in the records of this Court a product of high literary merit. If the Court below erred in interpreting existing law it devolved upon this Court to discern the deviation and make the necessary adjustment.

Standing on the high plateau of review, isolated from the smoke of battle of nisi prius, and unencumbered by contending parties importuning for rapid decisions, it could be assumed that this Court would, with the employment of meditation and the application of reflection, repair the rent in the fabric of *stare decisis* and once again make whole the pattern of justice under the law. But this Court failed to assume that burden. It made no attempt to explain why in February, 1953, it resolved an issue, which we will shortly consider, one way; and, today, decided the same, identical issue in a wholly different way. In February, 1953, this Court expounded in convincing language that under *certain circumstances* the word "war" does not mean war. Today it declares that in exactly the *same circumstances*, it does mean war. In February, 1953, it announced that the Korean conflict was not a war. Today it announces that it was a war. Non-lawyers who might try to reconcile our decision of 1953 with the decision of this moment would not corrugate their brows one-half as much as lawyers and judges who will devote

[*1]It is an interesting, if not disturbing, phenomenon, that this is the third time in as many months that a Court of Common Pleas has reversed the Supreme Court of Pennsylvania without arousing any expression of concern on the part of this Court. The other cases are Commonwealth v. Green, 387 Pa. 515, 128 A.2d 577, and Clewell v. Pummer, 384 Pa. 515, 121 A.2d 459.

themselves to the same Herculean effort of attempted reconciliation. Let us now proceed to the objective facts in the litigation at hand.

• • •

There is only one question before us, and that is: Did Francis Thomas, Jr., die as the result of an act of war?

It would be difficult to conceive of a more realistic and genuine war scene than the one in which Francis Thomas met his death. As a United States Marine engaged in action against enemy forces in Korea, while his company was under heavy mortar and artillery fire, he advanced on the foe with rifle and grenade and was struck down by an exploding enemy grenade. There is no doubt that Francis Thomas was killed in battle. Was that battle-death the kind of death which was excluded from the insurance policy of which the plaintiff in this case is the beneficiary? The answer to that question is not to be found alone amid the smoke and acrid smell of gunpowder on the bleak, cold Korean hill which witnessed the heroic and glorious death of Francis Thomas. It is to be found also in the carpeted, comfortable, and commodious offices of the Metropolitan Life Insurance Company where its skilled, expert, and experienced lawyers drafted the contract which was to become the insurance policy purchased by 17-year-old Francis Thomas. What did these lawyers have in mind when they said that their company would not pay double indemnity in the event the insured came to his death as the result of an act of war? What language did they employ in expressing the contingency under which the company would not be required to pay the additional sum stipulated in the policy? They knew that under Article I, Section 8, Clause 11, of the United States Constitution, only Congress can declare war and that, therefore, a state of war can come into being only when the elected representatives of the people of the United States by suitable legislation so pronounce. Thus, in preparing the formal instrument which was to bind their master, the lawyers would naturally adopt formal language and we can only conclude that when they used the word "war" they could only mean war in its constitutional sense.

Was the Korean conflict, then, war in its constitutional sense?

The answer is No.

On February 20, 1951, the Committee on Foreign Affairs of the United States House of Representatives declared: "No declaration of war has been made by the Congress. The President has not proclaimed a state of war, nor have the North Korean or Chinese Communist authorities."

While very interesting, it is rather a profligate expenditure of words to discuss what is meant by war. We all know that there can be the taking of life, destruction of property, and draining of resources in rebellions, expeditions, insurrections and raids which suggest war and which certainly feature warlike activities, but when we speak constitutionally, *and a Court has no right to speak otherwise,* war can only mean a war *declared to be such by Congress.* And we know that Congress did not declare war on the foe in Korea. No matter how strange it might seem that the United States could have waged so serious a contest of arms as that which ensanguined the entire Korean Peninsula, and yet the contest not become a state of war, the fact still remains that Congress did not declare war—and only Congress can declare war. The Metropolitan Life Insurance Company's legal staff knew that when they expressed a certain contingency through the medium of the word "war," only a certain legal status could result from the use of that word, and the Metropolitan Life Insurance Company must be held accountable for the employment of that word in its formal and documentary sense. If the Metropolitan legal staff had wanted to exclude conflicts which were not constitutionally declared wars, they could have done this clearly, neatly, and easily. All they had to do was to add after the word, "war," the words "declared or undeclared." But they did not do this and we have no authority to excuse that omission by speculation or rationalization, or, least of all, on some arbitrary theory which saves the company from a voluntarily assumed contractual obligation.

What is war and what is not war has been decided by the Courts of the nation so often that no lawyer, or insurance policy drafter, can plead ignorance on the subject.

• • •

It is not for the courts to appraise a military situation and from it decide whether a state of war exists or does not exist. We do not have the facilities and certainly not the authority to count the divisions employed, ascertain the calibre of the guns in action, estimate the tanks in movement, calculate the intensity of the air power in the skies, and, from it all, decide in any given situation, if the United States is at war. We have only one measuring rod to use in determining whether a martial situation has reached the point of war, and that is when Congress declares that it has reached that point. For reasons which it is not for us to question or even to consider, Congress, in the exercise of its constitutional prerogatives, decided not to bring the Korean conflict within the boundaries of War. Are we now a super-Congress to say that, despite the fact that Article I, Section 8, Clause 11 of the Constitution was never employed in determination of the Korean conflict, we, the Supreme Court of Pennsylvania will nevertheless legislate that contest at arms into constitutional war? If so, where do we derive such authority?

Once this Court begins to decide what is war and what is not war, disregarding the clear and mandating language of the United States Constitution, chaos has thrust its head under the tent of governmental order and responsibility. In point of ineradicable fact and historical unbudgeability we decided only four years ago that we do not have the power. If it has sprouted in the quadrennium, who sowed the seed and where?

On February 14, 1953, in the case of Beley v. Pennsylvania Mutual Life Ins. Co., 373 Pa. 231, 95 A.2d 202, 205[4]* we solemnly and unequivocally declared that the Korean conflict was not war. Chief Justice Horace Stern, speaking for the Court, said with noonday clarity:

"The existence or nonexistence of a state of war is a political, not a judicial, question, and it is only if and when a formal declaration of war has been made by the political department of the government that judicial cognizance may be taken thereof."

We, therefore, decided in the Beley case, in 1953, that the Korean expedition was not war. Why do we now, in 1957, say it was war? The revered United States Supreme Court Justice Jackson, commenting on the fact that the parties in a certain case[5]† had changed positions after the legal action had been begun, made the unique observation: "In this Court the parties changed positions as nimbly as if dancing a quadrille." Paraphrasing Justice Jackson, I would say that this Court has demonstrated the same terpsichorean agility in taking up today a position diametrically opposed to the one it held four years ago. How are lawyers to advise their clients on their rights under insurance policies when the highest Court in the Commonwealth,

*[4]The United States Supreme Court denied certiorari, 1953, 346 U.S. 820, 74 S. Ct. 34, 98 L. Ed. 346.

†[5]Orloff v. Willoughby, 345 U.S. 83, 73 S.Ct. 534, 537, 97 L. Ed. 842.

on that subject, emulates the inconstancy of the weathervane and the irresoluteness of Cynthia of the minute?

• • •

But argue as much as the Majority may, about the Communist attack on United States sovereignty converting the United Nations action in Korea into an American war, no amount of argumentation, no line of reasoning, no type of logic can cut away the mountain range in its path that this very Court planted on February 14, 1953, when it proclaimed, in whatever tones of thunder a sovereign Court can proclaim, that:

"It is clear that the action being waged in Korea is *not* a 'war' within what may be termed the 'constitutional' or 'legal' sense of that term."

If the Majority here had said that it was overruling the Beley decision, then at least it would be consistent with what it is doing in the present case; and, in any event, the legal profession would know in what direction the weathervane was pointing. But this Court does not overrule the Beley decision. It stands by it, and attempts to distinguish it from the case at bar. But in doing so, it undertakes the hopeless task of differentiating between Roland and Oliver. Thus, it points out that in the Beley insurance policy the exclusionary phrase read: "time of war," whereas in the Thomas policy the exclusionary phrase reads: "act of war." Is that a difference? The Majority says that Beley was not killed in time of war (Korean), but that Thomas was killed by an act of war (still Korean). Would Aristotle approve of that kind of logical differentiation?

It is to be noted that in his whole admirable exposition of the issue involved in the Beley case, Chief Justice Stern did not once mention the phrase "time of war", except to quote it from the insurance policy. He did not analyze or define the word "time" as it appears in the phrase "time of war." He considered and discussed only the word "war," which, obviously, is the catalytic agent in the whole alembic of discussion. In the very first sentence of his opinion, Chief Justice Stern asked: "Is the present struggle in Korea a 'war' within the meaning of that term as employed in a certain life insurance policy?" Speaking for the Court he answered that question No. Why does the Court today answer the same question Yes?

In affirming the lower Court's decision denying payment of insurance benefits to the plaintiff, this Court argues that Francis Thomas's death was an "act of war" and thus falls within the interdicting provision in the policy which uses the same phrase. We have seen that so far as the courts are concerned, the word "war" means constitutional war; it means congressionally declared war. It cannot mean anything else. We said so on February 14, 1953. The Constitution of the United States says so. Do we need any higher authority? Thus, the phrase "act of war" must be read "act of constitutional war." Since the Korean conflict is not a constitutionally declared war, that fact should of itself demonstrate that the exclusionary provision in the policy is inoperative. However, since the Majority discusses at length the phrase "act of war," candor requires comment on the Majority's use of those words.

We know what "war" is. What is "act"? Standing alone, the word "act" is practicaly rudderless unless, of course, we are referring to a law passed by a legislative body or the division of a stage play. But the word "act," when it forms part of a phrase, can be one of a thousand things. It can be an act of kindness, an act of mercy, an act of anger, an act of charity, an act of reprisal, an act of bankruptcy, an act of sale, the act of a human being, the act of a chimpanzee, the act of an elephant, the act of a mosquito, but in each instance where the act is the product of something else, it is the something else which dominates the phrase. In "act of war" it is "war" which controls and gives substance to the entire phrase. The base of the prepositional phrase, "war" is what imparts significance and precision to the antecedent noun, "act."

As the base of the prepositional phrase under discussion, "war" thus becomes the foundation, the bedrock of the pyramid of meaning; it is the granitic bottom which upholds the entire superstructure. Therefore, it is apparent that the cardinal error in the Majority's Opinion is that it hinges the explanation of its decision on the word "act," when the emphasis, of course should be on the word, "war." The Majority pitches its tent of reasoning on the apex of the pyramid, instead of on the firm ground which supports the pyramid. Naturally, resting on so precarious a scaffolding, the whole rationalization of the Majority must fall when touched by the lance of logic or jostled by the probing rule of grammatical analysis.

But the Majority will say that it is not dividing "act" from "war," and that it uses the entire phrase "act of war" as one indivisible concept. But what concept does the Majority have in mind? In narrating how Francis Thomas was killed, the Majority describes act of war in the sense of an incident of warfare. And there is a meaning as wide as the ocean between war and warfare.

• • •

I have said that "act of war" has many meanings, and unless the phrase is used precisely and in a setting which identifies the significance intended by the phrase, inextricable confusion will result. For instance, in its discussion, the Majority uses the phrase "act of war" in many varied ways but it attempts to synonymize them all into one identical meaning. Thus, it speaks of the sinking of the Lusitania as an act of war; it speaks of Pershing's expedition into Mexico as an act of war; it speaks of Thomas's death as an act of war. These three episodes differ as much from one another as if they happened on three individual planets. The sinking of the Lusitania was a *casus belli*; the Pershing Punitive Expedition was a reprisal which did not eventuate in war; the killing of Thomas was an incident of warfare. The Majority speaks of the bombing of the Panay, the explosion of the U.S.S. Maine, the Boxer Rebellion in China, the air attack on Rotterdam, and the destruction of Warsaw, all as acts of war. But certainly those acts of war cannot be equated with the act of war made up of the isolated incident of one soldier's hurling a grenade against another soldier on the battlefield of an undeclared war. In the Pershing Punitive Mexican Expedition, and the Panay, Maine, Lusitania, Rotterdam, and Warsaw events, the actions of sovereign nations were involved. Those acts of war can have no possible relationship to hand-to-hand combat between two soldiers.

The Majority Opinion states:

"Justice Musmanno in his *** [concurring] opinion in the Beley case, supra, made a clear distinction between a 'state of war' and 'an act of war', when he said (373 Pa. 231, 95 A.2d 216): 'There can be acts of war without there being a state of war. Beley was killed by an act of war but not in a state of war.'"

When the writer of this Opinion made the above quoted statement he was not distinguishing between an "act of war" and a "state of war." He was showing that an act of war may occur *during* a state of war as well as *outside* a state of war. Thus, as I have already shown, the sinking of the United States destroyer Reuben Jones was an act of war, but it did not occur *during* a state of war. The bombing of Pearl Harbor was an act of war but it did not occur during a state of war. The fact that I stated that Beley was killed by an act of war establishes that I regarded this particular act of war (and the phrase was here used in the sense of an incident of warfare) was *not* excluded by the insurance policy. I maintained that the act of war which killed Beley did not deprive his mother of benefits under the insurance policy, as I maintain today that the act of war which killed Thomas does not deprive his father of benefits under the insurance policy. I agreed with the Majority in the Beley case because it said that the Korean conflict was not a war and it authorized payment of insurance payments, and I disagree with the Majority in the case of today because, contrary to what it said four years ago, it now holds that the Korean conflict was a war.

The Majority says further in its opinion:

"If it is true that Beley was killed by an act of war, then it would seem that Francis R. Thomas, Jr., the Insured in the instant case, also met his death by an act of war. Both met their death in Korea by enemy action."

I agree with this statement completely, and the inevitable question follows: If this Court found that Beley was killed by an act of war and it *affirmed* the payment of insurance benefits, why does it now, finding that Thomas was also killed by the same kind of an *act of war, deny* the payment of insurance benefits? How does the death of Thomas differ from the death of Beley? As the Majority well says: "Both met their death in Korea by enemy action." But how does the Majority explain the fact that in 1953 when it found that Beley was killed by enemy action, it authorized payment of insurance benefits, but today that it finds Thomas was killed by the same enemy action, it refuses payment of insurance? Where is the consistency? Where is the logic? Where is the law? Where is the justice? The lawyer for the plaintiff in this case has my earnest sympathies because I can understand to what straits he will be put in trying to explain to his client (who, of course, must know about the Beley case), why the Beley family was entitled to insurance benefits but the Thomas family is not entitled to insurance benefits, when the Supreme Court of Pennsylvania specifically says and admits that both boys "met their death in Korea by [the same] enemy action."

To allow the defendant insurance company in the case at bar to escape liability is to put a premium on contractual looseness. In the Beley case, Chief Justice Stern said [273 Pa. 231, 95 A.2d 205]:

"A policy of life insurance is a highly technical instrument, drawn up presumably with meticulous care by legal experts on behalf of the Insurance Company, and who not only intend to use all terms in their legal sense but know how to accomplish that result; it may be assumed, therefore, that if defendant had here meant to invest the term 'war' with a broader connotation than its 'constitutional' or 'legal' intendment, it would have effected this by the addition of words indicating such an intention, as, for example, 'declared or undeclared' war."

We thus ruled that if an insurance company prefers to use language which makes it liable under certain conditions, when it could by a slight modification exonerate itself from such liability, it uses such language at its peril. Why does that rule not apply in the present Thomas case?

If the Majority does not accept my view that the Thomas insurance policy does not exclude the payment of certain benefits when the insured is killed in an undeclared war, it certainly must agree, by the very length of its opinion, that there is some ambiguity in the policy as to what it actually means. Under those circumstances should not the policy be interpreted most favorably to the insured?

Of all contracts, the insurance policy should be the most clearly worded. When a person purchases a policy with benefits payable to those he loves, he wants to give to those endeared ones not a sword with which to fight a bitter and costly legal battle, but a vehicle in which they may ride over the lonely and rocky road he leaves behind him. It is for that reason that we have frequently said that—

"Where the terms of a policy are susceptible of different interpretations the construction most favorable to the insured should be the one adopted ** The reason for this is that the language of the policy is prepared by the insurer, presumably with the purpose in mind of protecting itself against future claims in regard to which it does not desire to accept liability." Snader v. London & Lancashire Indem. Co., 360 Pa. 548, 551, 62 A.2d 835, 836.

This fundamental principle of construction was reinforced by our statement in the Beley case that:

"Obviously the right of an insured to recover under a life insurance policy should not be left to depend upon the determination of a question not governable by any definite test either legal or factual; on the contrary, its terms and conditions should be interpreted according to some definite and uniform standard."

That definite and uniform standard we have established, namely, that war means war according to the Constitution. Why are we departing from that standard which is so simple, so just, and so fair? Why should the right of a beneficiary under an insurance policy have to depend upon commas, semi-colons and exhausting reasoning that might be applicable to an algebraic problem but hardly consonant with the simple duty of doing justice under a contract whose intent and purpose are clear?

I dissent from the decision of the Majority for the following reasons:

1. It deprives the plaintiff Francis Thomas, Sr., of a recovery to which he is entitled.

2. It accomplishes a retreat from a principle solemnly arrived at and solemnly announced.

3. It accomplishes the reversal of a previous decision without a specific statement to that effect.

4. It is a blow to the integrity of precedents.

5. It plays at ducks and drakes with the principle of stare decisis.

6. It throws a veil of perplexity, doubt and confusion over insurance contracts.

7. It gives to "war" a hydra-headed meaning.

8. It encourages the use by insurance-policy-drafters of ambiguous phrases.

9. It ignores a provision of the United States Constitution.

10. It presumes that the charter of the United Nations supersedes the authority of the United States Constitution.

Four cases decided in 1959-1965 added little to the substance of the arguments so extensively presented in the majority and minority opinions in *Thomas,* quoted at some length above.

In February, 1959 the Supreme Court of North Carolina decided the case of *Constance Zaytoun Lamar v. John Hancock Mutual Life Insurance Company*[20] on appeal from the Superior Court of Craven County. The decision of the lower court in favor of the insurance company was upheld by the Supreme Court, with a very brief statement:

> PER CURIAM.
>
> Upon the facts stipulated by the parties, the conclusion reached by the trial court follows as clearly as does the night follow the day. Citation of authority is not required to sustain the judgment below. Hence it is
>
> Affirmed.

The policy had used the phrase "in time of war, whether such war be declared or undeclared," and in the judgment of the North Carolina courts this definition included the Korean conflict.

Schneiderman v. Metropolitan Cas. Co. of N.Y.[21] was decided in 1961 by the Appellate Division, First Department, of the New York Supreme Court. The facts differed from those in earlier cases, as noted below. The headnotes are quoted as a summary of the opinion:

> 1. *Insurance*
>
> Death of photographer-journalist who was killed when jeep, in which he was traveling with a party exchanging wounded, was fired upon four days after warring nations had agreed to cease fire, was not "caused by war or any act of war" within scope of exclusionary clause of life policy.
>
> 2. *International Law*
> *War and National Defense*
>
> International law recognizes that war may be terminated by actual cessation of hostilities and the absence of a formal peace treaty is of no significance.
>
> 3. *Insurance*
>
> "War" as used in exclusionary clause of life policy refers to period of hostilities and not to a technical state of war which may exist after fighting has ended.
>
> 4. *Insurance*
>
> Court must consider life policy as a whole and construe it liberally to give effect to purpose for which it was written.
>
> 5. *Insurance*
>
> Rule requiring construction of any ambiguity against insurer has particular application where exclusions are involved.

The opinion of the court was delivered by Justice Eager with the concurrence of three justices, and the dissent of Justice Steuer.

The "war" in question involved extensive military and naval action commenced by the British, Israeli and French governments against the Egyptian government to seize control of the Suez Canal. The conflict began in October, 1956, and an agreement to cease fire became effective November 6, 1956. The insured's death occurred on November 10, after the cease-fire agreement. The insurance company claimed that, at the time of the insured's death, war or a state of war existed—the insured claimed that war, within the meaning of the policy, had ended.

Quotations from the opinion follow:

> [2] That a war may be terminated by the actual cessation of hostilities is recognized by authorities in international law and by judicial decision. While it is written in text books that a regular or normal way of ending a war is by a treaty of peace or by conquest and annexation, it is conceded by the authors that actual cessation of hostilities pending peace preliminaries may mark the ending of a war.
>
> • • •
>
> Of course, our ultimate aim here is to find and give effect to the intention of the parties in contracting for exclusion from coverage for death "caused by war or any act of war". The words used are to be taken and read in their plain and ordinary sense. "Such meaning must be given to the terms used as would be ascribed to them by the average man in applying for insurance and reading the language of the policy at the time it was written.
>
> • • •
>
> We are to take cognizance of the fact that an insurance policy is generally a contract with the average man who presumably is unfamiliar with the existence of a state of war from the strictly political, military and/or legal standpoint. Such a man would read the term war in a policy exclusory clause in the sense that the term is commonly used and understood in the every day expression rather than as used and understood in international relations or military affairs. Thus "[t]he common understanding of the meaning of 'war,' as related to its likeli-

hood to be the cause of death, and the interpretations given to the usage of such a term in the current of judicial history, would be controlling."

• • •

[3] "War, in the practical and realistic sense in which it is commonly used, refers to the period of hostilities and not to a technical state of war which may exist after the fighting has ended.

• • •

In the mind of the ordinary or average man, a war is considered at an end on the final cessation of hostilities following an armistice or cease fire looking toward complete peace. For example, a common expression, when the fighting stops, heard in the street or seen in the headlines, is the "War is over".

Consequently, in connection with the interpretation of private contracts, the courts have treated the actual cessation of hostilities as synonymous with the cessation of war.

• • •

Therefore, the term war when used in an exclusory clause of an insurance policy is generally construed as referring to the period of actual hostilities, that is, in the absence of context plainly having the effect of broadening the term beyond such limits. [*Bennion, Durham, Stinson, Beley* and *Leverett* were cited.]

Moreover, in limiting the meaning of the terms "war" and "act of war" as used in the exclusory clause to the meaning of war in its real and practical sense, we are giving effect to the apparent intention of the parties [*Davis* and *Gagliormella* were cited].

[4,5] In any event, we are bound to consider the policy as a whole and, on such consideration, construe it liberally to give effect to the purpose for which it was written.

• • •

The opinion continued with statement of the nature of special disability policies (like the one under consideration), and the company's obligation to use clear and unmistakable terms so that the insured could not be misled. The rule dictating construction of any ambiguity against the insurer has particular application where exclusions are involved. Here, the company used ambiguous terms, in the judgment of the court (*Thomas* and *Bennion* were cited).

> The uncertainty in the language used is chargeable to the company, and any doubt in the construction to be adopted must be resolved against it. Thus, reasonably, the exclusory clause should be limited in its application to a death occurring as a direct consequence of war. Here, the direct cause of death *was not the war or an act of war* but an *unexplained act of violence* following the ending of the war.
>
> • • •
>
> In view of the foregoing, we conclude that the plaintiff should have judgment against the defendant for $5,000 with interest from December 1, 1956, and with costs.
>
> Judgment for plaintiff against defendant for the sum of $5,000 with interest from December 1, 1956 and with costs. Settle order on notice.
>
> All concur except STEUER, J., who dissents in dissenting opinion.
>
> STEUER, Justice (dissenting).
>
> I dissent from the opinion of the majority. I am constrained to this conclusion not by any marked disagreement with the principles of law stated in the opinion but with their applicability to the facts likewise stated with accuracy, which I find unexceptionable. It is a correct statement of the law that the continuance of war as defined in the policy is not dependent upon the diplomatic or political arrangements made between the belligerent nations and that what is to be understood by the term is the period of actual hostilities. This period may be greater or less than the formal state of war originated by a declaration and terminated by a treaty or an armistice. Thus, it would be indisputable that a condition or an act of war existed at Pearl Harbor prior to any formal declaration, and the same is true if organized hostilities continue beyond the time that either or both of the belligerents have signified their intention to desist from such activities. The question is whether in fact they do so desist.

Justice Steuer pointed to the continuance of violence after the ceasefire, as evidenced by the fact that the insured was killed by fire from regular troops from a regularly maintained position.

> This could only mean that an act of war was being perpetrated by one of the belligerents contrary to its declared intention. As we have already seen, the declared intention is not the criterion. It is what is actually done.
>
> The controversy should be determined in favor of the defendant.

In November, 1962 the Appellate Division, Third Department of the New York Supreme Court announced its decision in the case of *Goodrich v. John Hancock Mut. Life Ins. Co. of Boston.*[22] The facts of the case and the relevant points of the decision were summarized in headnotes 1-4:

> 1. *Insurance*
> Korean conflict was a "war" within meaning of life policies which excluded, in one case, accidental death benefits where insured's death resulted from military service in time of war, and, in the other case, accidental death benefits if insured's death resulted directly or indirectly from state of war.
>
> 2. *Insurance*
> Question of meaning of wording in policies is primarily what was intent of parties at time of signing of insurance contract.
>
> 3. *Insurance*
> Insured's death as result of accidental discharge of carbine of fellow soldier, while insured was serving in Korean conflict, was a death resulting from "military service" within meaning of life policies which excluded accidental death benefits in case of death resulting from military service during war.
>
> 4. *Insurance*
> Contract of insurance is no different from any other contract, and, like other contracts, is to be construed according to sense and meaning of terms which parties have used, and if policies are clear their terms are to be taken and understood in their plain, ordinary and proper sense.

The Supreme Court, Special Term had entered an order and judgment granting the insurer's motion for summary judgment dismissing the complaint, and the beneficiary had appealed. The Supreme Court, Appellate Division held that the Korean conflict was a "war" within exclusionary provisions of the two policies, reversing the judgment of the lower court as to this cause of action. Judgment in a second cause of action, unrelated to the question of definition of "war," was affirmed.

The court relied on the earlier New York case, *Schneiderman,* with considerable quotation, and *Stanbery, Langlas, Lynch, Meadows* and *Christensen* were cited in support. The court was not prepared to follow the majority decision in *Beley*. The reasoning of the court presented no new arguments.

The Appellate Court of Indiana rendered a decision in July, 1965 in the case of *Marian Ford Stucker, Appellant, v. The College Life Insurance Company of America, Appellee.*[23] The Circuit Court, Morgan County had entered judgment adverse to the beneficiary, and the Appellate Court upheld this decision.

The headnotes are quoted as a summary of the Appellate Court opinion:

> 1. *Insurance*
> Where life policy excluded coverage for death resulting from "war" and defined "war" as meaning war, or any act of war, declared or undeclared, and insured, while serving in armed forces of United Nations, was killed as a result of wounds received in Korean conflict, his death resulted from "war" within meaning of exclusionary provision of policy.
>
> 2. *Insurance*
> Terms employed in an insurance contract must be understood and interpreted in their popular and ordinary meaning.
>
> 3. *Insurance*
> It is not proper function of Appellate Court to remake insurance contract for parties.

The opening portion of the opinion of the court dealt with matters not directly relevant to the definition of "war." The appellant claimed, and the court agreed, that the policy was made in the State of Colorado, and the appellee did not contest this. The parties differed, however, on the question of whether the law of Colorado governed the obligations of the appellee under the policy. A statute of Colorado[24] and a decision of the Colorado Supreme Court[25] were in question. (Omitting discussion of the statute) the effect of the *Pyramid* decision was discussed at some length. The appellant relied heavily on the construction which the court in that case had placed on the meaning of the war clause in the policy before it–namely, that the existence or nonexistence of a "state of war" is a political, and not a judicial, question, and that judicial cognizance of a "state of war" may be taken only when a formal declaration of war has been made by Congress. *Beley* was quoted in support of this holding.

The issue presented to the court was stated simply as follows:

> "Do the 'war clause' exclusions as set forth in the policy of insurance executed by appellee upon the life of Appellant's late husband apply in the case of death occurring from bullet wounds received by him while serving in the armed forces of the United Nations in the Korean Action?"
>
> Appellant and appellee confine themselves in their briefs exclusively to this sole question except for the point of which State law controls. We are then left to determine whether the "Korean Action", alleged in the amended complaint, was "war", declared or undeclared, as the term is used in said exclusion clause of appellee's policy. Appellant offers us no help on this particular question and makes no mention of it in the argument section of her brief except to say that with reference to the Korean Action the Congress of the United States has never declared it a war. Under the challenged allegations of appellant's amended complaint it is not necessary to find that the United States was at war; it is sufficient, in passing upon whether the amended complaint states a cause of action, to find whether, on October 16, 1952, a war existed between North Korea and South Korea (referred to in the amended complaint as the "Korean Action"). Much time and labor could be expended in setting forth herein, in detail, the factual situation which establishes quite clearly that on October 16, 1952, North Korea and South Korea were then actually at war with each other. Several cases contain extensive facts on this general issue to support this conclusion. [*Thomas, Stankus* and *Lynch* were cited.]
>
> Many State Courts of last resort have been called upon to interpret similar "war risk" clauses as that in the Pyramid case and, under the same circumstances, some have followed the

so-called constitutional interpretation as in the Pyramid and Beley cases. However, the majority have held that similarly worded clauses under like circumstances should be interpreted in their broad sense and that the Korean Conflict was a "war" within such clause. [*Langlas, Carius, Lynch, Thomas* and others were cited.]

In some recent cases the courts have dealt with war risk clauses having more similarity to the ones we are considering in that they contain the words "declared or undeclared" either following, preceding or defining the term "war" used in said clauses. All cases of this nature which we can find have interpreted the Korean Conflict as an "undeclared war" within the provision of said exclusions. [*Goodrich, Lamar, Wilkinson,* and *Zaccardo* were cited.]

Even if we were to concede, as appellant strongly urges, that we are bound by the holding of the Colorado Court in Pyramid Life Insurance Company v. Masch, supra, no benefit would be derived therefrom because that court specifically states that it was asked to take judicial notice that the engagements of "United States troops" in Korea constituted war. As we have heretofore pointed out, no such question is here before us.

[1] For this court to hold that the so-called "Korean Action" was not a war would be closing our eyes to the events of our times and to the world in which we live. The world of chivalry in conflict between nations ended abruptly with the infamous attack on Pearl Harbor. The progress of science in the art of war has so far advanced that any thought we may entertain that our nation would be allowed an opportunity to formally declare war is certainly burying our heads in the sand to reality.

Not only has the machinery of attacking another nation been refined to a point that has virtually disposed of warning, but the weapons of attack and their destructive power are so devastating as to be nearly incomprehensible. In this world of restlessness in every country, with our resources, both material and human, being used in every corner of the earth, and possibly in the near future into outer space, the law must recognize what we know as individuals. To say that the attack on Pearl Harbor, the action in Korea, the activities in Viet Nam are not wars, and that those killed were not killed by war, is saying, in effect, that war is not war.

Attacks without warning, so-called police actions throughout the world, American service men on every continent, are a fact of life and a part of our way of life, whether we approve or not.

> Freedom for mankind is challenged every minute of every day and its enemies are unconcerned with the formalities of yesterday and will resort to any means they feel necessary to accomplish their desired goal.
>
> The parties here agreed, as stated in the written contract of insurance entered into between them, that "war" means "war, declared or undeclared." We must give effect to what the parties expressly agreed upon and we fail to find any authority, and none has been called to our attention which authorizes us to disregard the express language of the parties, or place a strained interpretation thereon contrary to the intent of the parties expressed in words of common understanding and acceptation.

Sections [2] and [3] in the opinion restated the well-known principles of construing terms used in insurance contracts.

Finally, the court held that the insured's death was contributed to by the Korean action, which they held to be war.

Notes

1. (1) County Court of Allegheny County, Pa., No. 1393 (1951), unreported.
   (2) Superior Court of Pa., 90 A. 2d 597 (1952), 171 Pa. Super. Ct. 253; reversed judgment of County Court (1953).
   (3) Supreme Court of Pa., 95 A. 2d 202, 373 Pa. 231; affirmed Superior Court judgment, and denied rehearing (1953).
   (4) U.S. Supreme Court, cert. denied, 346 U.S. 820 (1953).
2. (1) Court of Common Pleas of Luzerne County, Pa., No. 907 (1951), unreported.
   (2) Superior Court of Pa., 90 A. 2d 589 (1952), 171 Pa. Super. Ct. 236; reversed judgment of County Court (1953).
   (3) Supreme Court of Pa., 95 A. 2d 221, 373 Pa. 270; affirmed Superior Court judgment and denied rehearing (1953).
   (4) U.S. Supreme Court. cert. denied, 346 U.S. 812 (1953).
3. 69 *Am. Life Conv. Legal Bull.* 52 (1953).
4. 15 C.C.H. Life Cases 507 (1952); Municipal Court for the

District of Columbia, Civil Division. Civil No. B 14259-51. June 5, 1952.

5. 112 F. Supp. 420 (1953); No. 14670 United States District Court, S.D. California C.D. May 20, 1953.
6. 98 A.2d 134 (1953); 26 N.J. Super. 498 (1953).
7. (1) District Court, Young County [Texas], not reported (1953).

   (2) Court of Civil Appeals of Texas, 256 S.W. 2d 674. Judgment of the District Court affirmed and rehearing denied (1953).

   (3) Supreme Court of Texas, 261 S.W. 2d 554; 152 Tex. Sup. Ct. Rep. 559. Judgment of Court of Civil Appeals reversed and rehearing denied (1953).

   (4) United States Supreme Court. 347 U.S. 928, cert. denied (1954).
8. No. 16089–B.H., 1 C.C.H. Life Cases 2d 757 (1953-1955).
9. 63 N.W. 2d 885 (1954); 245 Iowa 713 (1954).
10. 122 F. Supp. 246 (1954).
11. *Stankus v. New York Life Insurance Co.*, 44 N.E. 2d 687; 312 Mass. 366 (1942). The war in question was that between Germany and the United Kingdom, but not between Germany and the United States.
12. 124 F. Supp. 388 (1954).
13. 122 N.E. 2d 900 (1954); 331 Mass. 752 (1954).
14. 278 S.W. 2d 32 (1955), No. 29140, April 10, 1955.
15. 284 P. 2d 287 (1955); 46 Wash. 2d 713 (1955). Rehearing denied June 20, 1955.
16. 151 N.Y.S. 1018 (1956); 2 Misc. 2d 249 (1956).
17. 299 P. 2d 117 (1956); 134 Colo. 70 (1956).
18. 124 A. 2d 926 (1956); 20 Conn. Sup. 76 (1956).
19. 131 A. 2d 600 (1957); 388 Pa. 499 (1957), rehearing denied April 17, 1957.
20. 107 S.E. 2d 65 (1959); 249 N.C. 643 (1959).
21. 220 N.Y.S. 2d 947 (1961); 86 A.L.C. 119 (1961).
22. 234 N.Y.S. 2d 587 (1962); 17 App. Div. 2d 271 (1962).
23. 208 N.E. 2d 731 (1965); 139 Ind. App. 422 (1965).
24. 1953 Colo. Rev. Stat. Anno., Vol. 3, ch. 72, Art. 3, § 22, p. 957.
25. *Pyramid Life Insurance Company v. Masch.* 299 P. 2d 117 (1956); 134 Colo. 70 (1956).

3

THE CONFLICT IN SOUTHEAST ASIA

In 1971 two decisions were rendered involving insurance claims arising from the conflict in Vietnam—(1) *Julian D. Hammond, Sr., Plaintiff-Appellant v. the National Life and Accident Insurance Company, Defendant-Appellee*[1], and (2) *Christine Jackson v. North American Assurance Society of Virginia, Incorporated.*[2] The Court of Appeal, Third Circuit, Louisiana in the *Hammond* case, and the Supreme Court of Virginia in the *Jackson* case, held that "war" was to be defined in its legal sense. Since Congress had not declared war, the Vietnam conflict was not to be so considered. Thus the two decisions in 1971 followed the principle in *Beley* and *Harding* (1953) and *Pyramid* (1956).

Headnote 1 in the *Hammond* case summarized the facts and the decision:

> Insured who died as result of a fire while serving in the United States Naval Reserve aboard an aircraft carrier in the Gulf of Tonkin during Vietnam conflict was not, at time of death, enrolled in military, naval or associated service "in time of war" within war exclusionary clauses of life policies in absence of a formal declaration of war by the Congress and beneficiary was entitled to recover double indemnity accidental death benefits.

The relevant portions of the opinion of the court are quoted:

> We are unable to find any Louisiana jurisprudence expressly interpreting the phrase "in time of war" as contained in the exclusionary provisions in the life insurance policies with which we are here concerned. Other states have interpreted the phrase as relating to the Korean conflict with divergent results. Plain-

tiff relies upon the case of Beley v. Pennsylvania Mutual Life Insurance Company, 373 Pa. 231, 95 A.2d 202; and defendant relies upon Stanbery v. Aetna Life Insurance Company, 26 N.J. Super. 498, 98 A.2d 134.

In Beley, supra, the insured was killed in action in Korea in 1951 while serving with the U.S. Army; and the court held for the insured stating that there had never been a declaration of war by Congress; and that the existence or nonexistence of a state of war is a political and not a judicial question. The court, in emphasizing there had been more than 150 occasions between 1798 and 1945 in which our military forces were engaged in various countries, felt that to include conflicts or hostilities other than those formally declared by Congress would leave the insureds without any definite and uniform standard as to whether recovery was or was not possible.

The court in the Stanbery case, supra, gave the word "war" a non-technical meaning and denied recovery where the insured was killed in the course of duty in Korea in 1952.

It is well settled that in cases of ambiguity, policy provisions are construed most favorably to the insured and against insurer. Also, that limitations and exceptions to coverage of the policy must be clearly expressed, and in case of doubt are construed unfavorably to the insurer who drafted the policy. . . .

[1] In our opinion the exclusionary clauses in the policies were ambiguous, and that at the time of his death, Julian D. Hammond, Jr., was not enrolled in military, naval or associated service "in time of war" as stated in the exclusionary provisions of the two insurance policies in the instant case; and, therefore, plaintiff is hereby allowed to recover the additional sum of $3,000.00 under the double indemnity benefit provisions of the policies.

• • •

For the reasons assigned the judgment appealed is reversed, and judgment is rendered in favor of plaintiff, Julian D. Hammond, Sr., and against defendant, The National Life & Accident Insurance Company, in the sum of $3,000.00.

Costs in the district court and on appeal are assessed against defendant.

Reversed and rendered.

Rehearing was denied in the *Hammond* case, and the Louisiana Supreme Court refused review.

Mr. Alfred A. Mansour, attorney for the plaintiff-appellant, in correspondence with the author wrote that all appellate remedies having been exhausted,

> The attorney for the insurance company told me that he would have attempted to carry the case to the United States Supreme Court had that Court not refused to review similar cases involving the Korean War.

A few months after the decision in the Louisiana case, *Hammond v. National Life and Accident Insurance Company*, a similar case was decided in Virginia. *Christine Jackson v. North American Assurance Society of Virginia, Incorporated* was decided by the Supreme Court of Virginia on September 1, 1971. The Hustings Court of the City of Petersburg had entered judgment for the insurer and the beneficiary appealed. The Virginia Supreme Court reversed the decision of the lower court.

The single headnote stated:

> Term "war," as used in clause in life policy excluding death by war or any act of war or injury suffered while in military or naval service in time of war, means war in its legal sense; hence clause was not applicable to member of Army who was a member of the United States Army on active duty when he was killed in Vietnam in vehicle accident.

Quotation from the opinion of the court follows: [citing the dissenting opinion in *Bennion*]

> "[T]here is war in the legal sense, and in the material sense. Legal war exists when there is an interruption of all pacific relations between nations and an authorized contestation of armed forces by the constitutional authority of the nations, while material war is evidenced by the use of armed forces by the parties". . . .
>
> Our use of armed forces in Vietnam does not constitute war in the legal sense because Congress has not declared war against North Vietnam. U.S. Const. art. I, § 8. For the purposes of this opinion, we may assume that our use of armed forces there does constitute war in the material sense.
>
> The authorities differ sharply in construing the word war as used in exclusionary clauses of insurance policies. Some assign

the legal meaning, while others assign the material meaning. *See* Hammond v. National Life & Acc. Ins. Co., 243 So.2d 902 (La.App. 1971); cases collected in Annot. 36 A.L.R.2d 1018 (1954), 145 A.L.R. 1464 (1943), 137 A.L.R. 1263 (1942); 1A J.A. and J. Appleman, Insurance Law and Practice § 561 (1965); H. Krueger and L. T. Waggoner, The Life Insurance Policy Contract § 18.6 (1953).[1*] We construe "war" in the exclusionary clause before us to mean war in its legal sense and, therefore, reverse the judgment appealed from.

We do not bottom our holding on the concept that courts may not take judicial notice that war exists until Congress declares war. *See* Pyramid Life Ins. Co. v. Masch, 134 Colo. 70, 299 P.2d 117 (1956). And we do not bottom our holding on ease of decision, though we recognize the difficulty of determining whether certain armed confrontations amount to material wars—e.g., our involvement in Lebanon in 1958 and in the Dominican Republic in 1962—and the difficulty of determining when a material war begins. Knowing that companies have issued policies with clauses excluding coverage in time of war, "declared or undeclared", *see e.g.*, Goodrich v. John Hancock Mut. Life Ins. Co., 17 App.Div.2d 271, 234 N.Y.S.2d 587 (1962), we could not confidently expect to avoid for long our decision whether this country is engaged in a material war in Vietnam.

Nor have we decided as a general proposition that the Vietnamese conflict is not war. Whether or not that conflict qualifies as a war in other contexts is quite beside the point "if the word war, as used in the contract [policy], was intended by the parties to mean a state of war which commenced only with a formal declaration by Congress ***. In construing and interpreting the contract between the parties, it is our function and duty to ascertain and effectuate their lawful intention. In so doing, we should place ourselves in the position of the parties when the contract was made, consider the purposes, the subject

*1Several of the cases referred to in the text involved the Korean conflict in the early 1950's. Only Hammond v. National Life & Acc. Ins. Co., *supra,* involved Vietnam. The conflicting views are fully set forth in the majority and dissenting opinions in Beley v. Pennsylvania Mutual Life Ins. Co., 373 Pa. 231, 95 A.2d 202 (1953), involving substantially the same question as that before us, and New York Life Ins. Co. v. Bennion, *supra,* involving a somewhat different question. A text writer far surpasses the acerbity of the dissenting judges. 1A J.A. and J. Appleman, Insurance Law and Practice § 561 at 381 (1965).

matter, and the circumstances under which their minds met." New York Life Ins. Co. v. Bennion, *supra* 158 F.2d at 264-265.

Since the word war has different meanings, an established rule may suffice to supply the parties' intention to refer to war in its legal sense: If language used in an insurance policy is susceptible of two meanings, one of which will permit recovery and the other will not, the language should be construed most favorably to the insured. *See* National Fire Ins. Co. v. Dervishian, 206 Va. 563, 145 S.E.2d 184 (1965).

The Insurance Company argues, however, that it did not bargain to insure against the hazards of armed conflicts. But nothing in the exclusionary language "while in military or naval service in time of war" ties the exclusion to combat-connected hazards. The language purports to exclude all accidents to insured servicemen during time of war, whether or not the accidents are combat-connected or service-connected and whether or not they happen in the combat zone.

We doubt that the parties intended to bargain against coverage for any accident befalling Cook while in military or naval service, provided a court should declare that the United States was then engaged in a material war. Rather, we believe it reasonable to conclude that the parties intended to bargain against coverage only in case of an announced and definite state of war—war in its legal sense.

We reverse the judgment appealed from and enter final judgment for Christine Jackson.

Reversed and final judgment.

Notes

1. 243 S. 2d 902 (1971); rehearing denied (1971).
2. 183 S.E. 2d 160 (1971); 212 Va. 177 (1971).

4

ARTICLES IN PROFESSIONAL JOURNALS

Reviews and journals published by university law schools, bar associations and insurance organizations in the period since World War II have contained a number of articles dealing with the definition of the word "war" contained in life insurance contracts, in judicial decisions rendered during that period. Several of these articles in 1945-1947 were based on cases involving the period before the declaration of war preceding World War II; a much larger number in 1953-1957 related to the Korean conflict; and two articles (as of July, 1975) related to the Vietnam conflict. A few articles dealt with the definition of termination of war, but in most cases the beginning of war was involved.

Assuming that many readers do not have enough time to consult all these cases and that, even with sufficient time, they may not have access to completely stocked law and insurance libraries, it appears to be useful to offer summaries and in some cases extensive quotations from the professional articles.

There are many articles relating to decisions in war-time insurance cases, but only those which contain discussion of the definition of war in such cases are included below.

A. *Chronological Outline of Articles*

World War II

The Japanese attack on Pearl Harbor on December 7, 1941 did not constitute war.

Sumaha (1945)[1]; *Yale Law Journal* (1947)[2]

---

[1]The full title and reference to each article is included in Section B, preceding the summary or the quotation.

[2]When no individual is named as author, the reference to the periodical is used.

The Japanese attack on Pearl Harbor on December 7, 1941 constituted war.

Borchard (1947); *Minnesota Law Review* (1947); Brown (1948); Abercrombie (1949)

Cessation of hostilities marked the end of war.

Price (1946); *Minnesota Law Review* (1947); Brown (1948); Drury (1948)

Korean Conflict

The Korean conflict did not constitute war.

Billings (1952); Serino (1953); *Albany Law Review* (1953); Kitzmiller (1953); *Miami Law Quarterly* (1953); Brandon (1953).

The Korean conflict constituted war.

Smith, Calvin E. (1952); *New York University Law Review* (1953); Trethway (1953); *George Washington Law Review* (1953); *West Virginia Law Review* (1953); Wheeler (1953); Anderson (1953); Bennett (1953); Short (1953); Creveling (1953); Charles (1953-1954); Cody (1954); *Vanderbilt Law Review* (1954); Marshall (1954); Kleiman (1957); *Fordham Law Review* (1957).

Cessation of hostilities did not mark end of war.

Smith, W. Clancy (1952).

Vietnam Conflict

Two articles–Albus (1972) no definition of war; Crain (1972) "common meaning" of word "war" is best.

B. *Summaries and Quotations*
(in chronological order)

1. Sumaha, Unwar J. Insurance–death "resulting from war" construed. Savage v. Sun Life Assurance Co. of Canada, 57 Federal Supplement 620 (Louisiana 1944), *Boston University Law Review,* v. 25, June 1945, pp. 289-291.

   (Held that the Pearl Harbor attack on December 7, 1941 was not war in absence of declaration by Congress.)

2. Price, Paul E. War and aviation exclusion clauses. *Insurance Law Journal,* v. 1946, September 1946, pp. 624-629.

   (Held that end of World War I, in the ordinary, lay sense, occurred at the cessation of hostilities. Unanswered questions still remain.)

3. [No author] Date of war inception as determinant of lia-

bility in life insurance contracts. *Yale Law Journal,* v. 56, April 1947, pp. 748-752.

> [Held that a declaration by Congress is needed to initiate a war. Determination of the existence of a state of war may be the key issue in contract interpretation, particularly if—as in the present case—the question had not been considered when the policy was written.]

What the contracting parties understood by "war" is of course the basic issue in these cases. The difficulty is that the policies contain no explicit expression of intent. In its absence, the courts have embarked on conceptual discussions of the "legal" meaning of the word. Just how the conclusions on this point have fitted into the courts' reasoning, however, is not entirely clear. If combined with the tacit presumption that the parties contracted with the legal word content in mind, determination of the legal inception date will itself decide the entire case. On the other hand, where the legal connotation of the word differs from the lay or factual meaning, it will also be relevant to show an ambiguity calling for construction in favor of the insured. In any event, the role of the "legal" meaning of war as only one proposition of a syllogism should be kept in mind in the ensuing discussion.

Writers on international law agree that a declaration of war has been the exception rather than the rule and is not necessary to the existence of war.[18*] There is a sharp disagreement, however, as to what acts short of a declaration constitute war.[19*] Some authorities, pointing to the many hostile acts that have not resulted in war,[20*] contend that war can exist only when aggression is coupled with intent to create a state of war.[21*] Others deplore the intention theory and deny that hostile action can be anything but war.[22*] Under either theory, it would seem that the United States and Japan were at war as of December 7.

• • •

Congressional determination need not be by a formal declaration of war, however, to command the notice of American courts.[29*]

[Neither action by Congress nor by the President prior to the Congressional declaration can be characterized as a formal recognition of a state of war with Japan.]

*Footnotes 18-22, 29 omitted.

The word "war" then has more than a single meaning. The court in the instant case resolved the ambiguity by declaring that the parties did not intend "to use the word war in the technical sense of a formally declared war."[46*] But this is too glib an assumption. Intent cannot be found by fiat. It is equally plausible to argue that Captain Bennion believed undeclared armed conflict to be one of the occupational hazards for which an extra premium was required. So also it is reasonable to assert that the insurance company lawyers, in drawing up the contract, were aware of the legal connotations attached to the word "war." This is not to argue that such conclusion is inescapable, but rather that it is as reasonable as that reached in this case. If this be granted, it follows that the words used were ambiguous—a conclusion bolstered by the fact that four courts had already held contrary to the Tenth Circuit.[47*]—and that the policy should have been construed in favor of the insured.[48*] Insurance company draftsmanship would still not bear too onerous a burden in excepting the risk of death resulting from armed conflict lacking a formal war label; other insurers have been more explicit on this same issue.[49*] Nor would it have involved the foresight of a seer; the history of our relations with other nations has not been devoid of such incidents.[50*]

4. Borchard, Edwin. When did the war begin? *Columbia Law Review,* July 1947, pp. 742-748.

   [Held that the attack on Pearl Harbor constituted war, and that war may be deduced from circumstances as a fact, in the absence of congressional delegation.]

It appears that under American law war or peace are the only political conditions recognized. If there is no war, a state of peace exists. If Pearl Harbor was not an act of war it must have been a friendly gesture—a peculiar act in view of the hostile conduct of the parties beginning at least with the Atlantic Conference and President Roosevelt's note to Japan of August 17, 1941.

How can it be determined whether a particular status is that of a state of war or a state of peace? The courts correctly decide that this is determined by the political department, although the courts may take judicial notice of historical facts. Collating the evidence from the political

---

*Footnotes 46-50 omitted.

department, we begin with President Roosevelt's message to Congress, December 8, 1941. In that message he stated that the state of war began "since the unprovoked and dastardly attack by Japan on Sunday, December 7 [1941]." It was at first asserted by the plaintiff that this meant that the state of war began after the attack, according to the President's own words. Also it will be recalled that Commissioner Fly testified before the Senate Investigating Committee that peace prevailed before the attack but not thereafter.[10*]

Apart from the President's message and the declaration of war which, notwithstanding the appellate opinion in the *Pang* case,[11*] was *not* contrary to the President's request, the Congressional declaration showed that war had existed since the attack by Japan December 7. Congress has considered that the casualties of Pearl Harbor were incurred during World War II as evidenced by the wording of numerous statutes.[12*] There was also in existence a presidential determination that war had begun: President Roosevelt had in an Executive Order of December 7 proclaimed the Japanese to be "alien enemies," in view of the fact that the United States had been invaded that day.[13*] Evidence was also available that the Department of State regarded the war as having begun December 7, 1941.[14*] The statements made by Congressmen on December 8 before the declaration of war all had assumed that war was in existence,[15*] and a subsequent Executive Order[16*] had assumed that World War II extended from December 7, 1941, to a date to be determined by the treaty of peace. In addition, there were in existence the "war warnings" issued November 27, 1941, which contemplated an attack such as actually took place, although no such devastation was expected.[17*] Besides, President Roosevelt during the campaign of 1940, while promising peace, had also promised that aggression would be repelled and that peace would be kept "except in case of attack."[18*]

The Supreme Court itself would seem to have indicated that, in its opinion, the Pearl Harbor attack meant war by the reasoning in *Duncan* v. *Kahanamoku*.[19*] All four opinions rendered in that case assume that the attack of Dec. 7, 1941 transformed the Hawaiian Islands into a center of active war.[20*] Furthermore, the Navy Department had stated: "events in the war which began on Sunday, De-

*Footnotes 10-20 omitted.

cember 7, 1941,"[21*] and "In one flash, the attack on Pearl Harbor had settled all that, and the war was on."[22*]

Judge Tillman Johnson, of the United States district court, had stated in his opinion in the *Bennion* case that he did not know whether the parties to the contract of insurance had had in mind "constitutional war" or "war in fact."[23*] Actually, that reasoning, logically followed, would decide the case in favor of the insurance company because in other cases it had been established that the clause "war or an act incident thereto" covered any kind of war. Judge Johnson doubtless meant by "constitutional war" a war declared by Congress. However, war in this country can also exist by act of invasion and no act of Congress is required. The President alone has power to repel an invasion of the United States, and there is evidence that President Roosevelt so assumed. To be sure, it is not always easy to determine that a particular act of war creates a state of war. But there can be no doubt that the Pearl Harbor attack was the first act in a state of war, the hostilities in which did not end until August, 1945. Contrary to Circuit Judge Huxman's dissenting view,[24*] the word "war" is unambiguous, even though it may be difficult to tell whether a particular engagement involves war or not. In this instance we had two declarations of war by the Japanese, one two hours and forty minutes after the commencement of the attack, and one that night, which indicate that Japan interpreted its act as one of war. We also have an acceptance of the Japanese challenge by Congress on December 8, 4:10 P.M. Thus the question naturally arises: Why were these declarations of war made? The answer is that no declaration of war was necessary either on the Japanese side or on the American. The Supreme Court had stated in the *Prize Cases,*

> "If a war is made by invasion of a foreign nation, the President is not only authorized but bound to resist force by force. He does not initiate the war, but he is bound to accept the challenge without waiting for any special legislative authority. And whether the hostile party be a foreign invader or states organized in rebellion, it is none the less a war, although the declaration of it be '*unilateral*'. . . . However long may have been its previous conception, it nevertheless sprung forth from the parent brain, a Minerva in the full panoply of *war*. The President was bound to meet it in the shape it presented itself,

*Footnotes 21-24 omitted.

without waiting for Congress to baptize it with a name; and no name given to it by him or them could change the fact."[25*]

Article I, Section 10, of the Constitution of the United States provides that "no state shall without the consent of Congress . . . engage in war unless actually invaded or in such imminent danger as will not admit of delay." This provision shows that the framers of the Constitution recognized that a state may be compelled to engage in war by reason of invasion, without any action whatever by Congress. It is common knowledge that war may exist without a declaration thereof; in fact, many instances could be produced to show that a failure to declare war is not exceptional. It has been stated in the case of *Dole v. Merchants Mutual Marine Insurance Co.*:

> "War is an existing fact, and not a legislative decree. Congress alone may have power to declare it beforehand, and thus cause or commence it. But it may be initiated by other nations, or by traitors; and then it *exists,* whether there is any declaration of it or not. It may be prosecuted without any declaration: or Congress may, as in the Mexican war, declare its *previous* existence. In either case it is the fact that makes 'enemies,' and not any legislative Act."[26*]

Judge Huxman was not fortunate in the illustrations he cited to support his contention that the word "war" was ambiguous and that it therefore might mean a "declared" war. Even assuming that "war or an act incident thereto" could mean either act of war or state of war, it could not by any stretch of the imagination mean "declared war." One could not import such a meaning into a contract which was plain on its face.[27*]

The four cases previously mentioned which had decided in favor of the widow and against the insurance company emphasizing the commencement of war by "declaration," disregarded the proposition that war may be commenced by "determination" and that there was plenty of evidence that the President had determined that the war began December 7, 1941.[28*]

Judge Huxman had thought that the invasion of Vera Cruz did not involve war. John Bassett Moore, in handing the prize of the American Philosophical Society to Quincy Wright for a study on the "Control of American Foreign

*Footnotes 25-28 omitted.

Relations," ridiculed the notion that 300 persons could be killed in hostilities in the absence of war. Mr. Moore on that occasion stated:

> "In reality the word 'war' comprehends two meanings. It denotes (1) acts of war, and (2) the international condition of things called a 'state of war.' Acts of war do not always or necessarily develop into the general international condition of things called a state of war, but they are nevertheless war and involve the 'making' of war in a legal sense. The fact is notorious that in many instances hostilities or war *de facto* have long preceded the formal declaration of war, and that when the declaration was made it was regarded as relating back to the time when hostilities began."
>
> [The remainder of the quotation includes discussion of the Vera Cruz incident.]

Moreover, the Boxer Rebellion,[30*] the Filipino Insurrection,[31*] and the Pershing expedition,[32*] were all found by American courts to have involved a state of war. In England, when the Executive refused to declare himself, it was held that the hostilities between China and Japan after 1937 involved a state of war.[33*] In addition, in American history we find that two battles, Palo Alto and Resaca de la Palma, were fought in the Mexican War before there was any declaration of war by Congress, and it appears that the casualties of those engagements were later regarded by Congress as victims of the war.[34*] It is usual in this country for Congress to declare that a state of war exists, implying that the state of war commenced some time prior to the declaration. In the Spanish-American War the declaration was expressly dated back four days,[35*] and in the Pearl Harbor case, while the declaration was not dated back to a particular day, it was dated back to a particular event which occurred on a day certain. Also hostilities may be unilateral only, and may indicate the war-like intent with which they were conducted. Furthermore, it had been held before December 7, in previous litigation concerning the war clauses of insurance policies, that the war need not involve the deceased's nation and another, but a war involving third countries only to which the insured's death is attributable will bring the clauses into operation.[36*]

It thus appears that war may be deduced from the circumstances as a fact and may exist independently of a declaration of war by Congress. The declaration, as in the

---

***Footnotes 30-36 omitted.**

Pearl Harbor attack, may serve the political purpose of uniting a disunited people, or it may be only necessary to authorize the commencement of hostilities against another country where that other country has done little to justify hostilities by the United States. The *Panay* case involved a disavowal of hostile intent by Japan, duly accepted by this country, and the declaration of war against Germany April 6, 1917, involved a response to equivocal acts which might or might not be acts of war. The Pearl Harbor attack can without equivocation be assumed to have been intentional, and to have started a war which all parties understood and acted upon.

5. [No author] Insurance–war risk exclusion clauses–meaning of the term "war." *Minnesota Law Review,* v. 32, December 1947, pp. 74-76.

   [Held that the term "war" used in exclusionary clauses of life insurance policies should be given the meaning that common speech imports, unless it is obvious that it was intended to be used in a technical sense.]

6. Brown, Wendell J. War clause of the next war. *Insurance Law Journal,* v. 1948, May 1948, pp. 382-394.

   [Held that the term "war" is to be interpreted as a term "of common speech and common parlance." Three cases–*Stinson, Durham* and *Ziegler*–establish the law applicable to the terminology used, in situations arising after unconditional surrender and before the formal declaration of termination of the war.]

7. Drury, Arthur P. Ambiguity in war clauses. *Insurance Law Journal,* v. 1948, September 1948, pp. 738-743.

   [Held that there is inherent difficulty in construction of the term "war." It is highly desirable that war clauses be unambiguous. Whether or not such a result can be attained is subject to some question.]

8. Abercrombie, Howard. Life insurance–effect of military service and war clauses. *Arkansas Law Review,* v. 3, Fall 1949, pp. 475-478.

   [Held that delineating "war" by formalities has the advantage of precision, but the courts can hardly go astray by noticing what everybody else knows, i.e., that the war is "on" or the war is "over."]

9. Smith, Calvin E. The meaning and effect of military service and war exception clauses in life insurance policies. *Duke Bar Journal,* v. 3, Fall 1952, pp. 11-20.

[Held that the Korean conflict is a United Nations' policing action which has the length, breadth and scope of a full-scale war. If the few jurisdictions which have taken a legalistic view of "war" clauses stand by this approach and multiply their numbers to a considerable extent and more cases find their way into court, it is inevitable that insurance companies are going to suffer and be forced to alter their policy provisions, expressing clearly their intentions.]

10. Billings, Robert B. Of war clauses. *Insurance Law Journal,* v. 1952, December 1952, pp. 793-806.

    [Held that today opinion is conflicting as to whether the Korean conflict is a war or not. The weight of authority exists to the effect that it is war. "On principle, it does not appear to me to be a war, and I venture to predict that our highest court will so hold when the issue is squarely presented to it."]

11. Smith, W. Clancy, Jr. Recent Decisions. Contracts–insurance–what is a "war." Harding v. Pennsylvania Mutual Life Ins. Co., . . . (1952). *University of Pittsburgh Law Review,* v. 14 (1952), pp. 122-125.

    [Commenting on *Harding,* held that the court should have found that a declared war still existed. If the President can terminate hostilities by proclamation, similarly a Presidential act committing troops to combat should operate to make a "result of war" clause effective.]

12. Serino, Rosemarie. Insurance–constitutional law–two recent cases, . . . *Catholic University of America Law Review,* v. 3, January 1953, pp. 60-62.

    [Held that insurance companies are faced with a difficult task in framing war exclusion clauses due to ambiguity in word usage. The remedy would be a uniform war clause with an unambiguous definition of war.]

13. J. W. R. Insurance–construction of war exclusion clauses. *Albany Law Review,* v. 17, January 1953, pp. 196-200.

    [Held that *Harding* will be followed by other courts because (1) of the usual tendency of courts to construe policies in favor of the insured, and (2) of an unwillingness to protect the insurer who neglects to provide for "undeclared wars" in his policy. Certainly, the foreseeable future will include many such wars.]

14. Kitzmiller, Howard L. Contract–interpretation of contract terms–meaning of "war" in termination clauses of insurance contract. *Dickinson Law Review,* v. 17, January 1953, pp. 172-175.

    [Held that the Korean conflict has been officially referred to as a war. The political department of government has made no determination that it is. The court cannot take judicial notice of a war until there has been some act or declaration creating or recognizing the existence of war, by the department of government clothed with the war-making power.]

15. [No author] Insurance–construction of war exclusion clause –Korean action. *Miami Law Quarterly,* v. 7, February 1953, pp. 261-263.

    [Held that the court's conclusion [in *Harding*] that the Korean conflict does not constitute war "seems to be well supported." Where private parties contract with reference to war, the term will be used in the legal sense unless the parties give it some other definition by contract.]

16. Brandon, Michael. 2. Is the Korean conflict "war"? Beley . . . and Harding . . . , New York Times, February 15, 1953, p. 4 (Pennsylvania Supreme Court, February 14, 1953). *International and Comparative Law Quarterly,* v. 2, April 1953, pp. 816-819.

    [Held that it is difficult to ascertain the intention of the parties, and the court was clearly justified in interpreting war in the strict legal sense.]

17. [No author] Insurance law–war clause exclusion–Korean action not a war. *New York University Law Review,* v. 28, April 1953, pp. 899-904.

    [The article contains discussion of *Beley* and *Harding* with no clear expression of the author's views.]

18. Trethway, John A. Insurance–contract–construction and operation–what is "war" within meaning of non-liability clause of life insurance policy. *Southern California Law Review,* v. 26, April 1953, pp. 328-331.

    [Held that the sounder view would be to give "war" its ordinary meaning. This is more likely to effect the intentions of the parties. Applying the technical meaning not only overlooks this intention but relies on inapposite authority by citing public law cases when the issue is construction of a private contract.]

19. G. W. H. War—hostilities in Korea—not war within meaning of insurance clauses. *George Washington Law Review,* v. 21, April 1953, pp. 657-660.

    [Held that *Beley* and *Harding* were erroneously decided, the strict construction against the insurer notwithstanding. The court failed to recognize in law that which exists in fact.]

20. G. M. S. Contracts—insurance—interpretation of the word "war." *West Virginia Law Review,* v. 55, June 1953, pp. 149-151.

    [Held that, although each line of decisions has received substantial support, the better view is contrary to that of *Beley* and *Harding.* It would seem that the Pennsylvania court erred in refusing to face economic realities. Interests of public policy militate strongly against its decision.]

21. Goldstein, Samuel J. The war clause in life insurance contracts. *Insurance Law Journal,* v. 1953, July 1953, pp. 458-478.

    [Mr. Goldstein was attorney for the plaintiff in *Beley,* tried before the Pennsylvania Supreme Court. The article contains a thorough review of *Beley* and *Harding* and preceding relevant cases.]

    The insurance carrier in the *Beley* case on June 22, 1953, filed a petition for writ of certiorari in the United States Supreme Court. However, it does not appear that any federal question is involved which would enable the Supreme Court to take jurisdiction, especially since no federal or constitutional question was raised during the proceedings or arguments. The Supreme Court has not yet acted upon the petition and it would appear to be a foregone conclusion that the writ of certiorari will be denied.

22. Corrigan, Bradford D. Insurance—"war exclusion clause" in life insurance policies. *Baylor Law Review,* v. 6, Fall 1953, pp. 111-114.

    [In comparing the decisions in *Meadows* and *Beley,* held that the question is one of contract law and the same set of facts will result in different conclusions in the various states as to a determination of what is "war."]

23. Brandon, Michael. 4. Weissman v. Metropolitan Life Insurance Company . . . Is the Korean conflict "war"? *International and Comparative Law Quarterly,* v. 2, October 1953, pp. 650-652.

[Held that *Weissman* serves to emphasize differences of judicial opinion concerning the nature of the Korean conflict for purposes of insurance policies. The authorities on both sides are impressive. It is welcome that *Beley* is apparently now to come before the Supreme Court.]

24. Wheeler, J. W. The war clause. *Insurance Law Journal,* v. 370, November 1953, pp. 727-737.

 [Mr. Wheeler was the attorney for the insurance company in *Meadows.* The present article was published prior to the decision in that case by the Texas Supreme Court. The full text of their opinion follows the article, at p. 737. Mr. Wheeler stated that "war is war, whether it be an aggressive war, a defensive war, a full-scale war, a constitutionally declared war or a nonconstitutionally declared war." The four Pearl Harbor cases failed to give proper recognition to the obvious intent of exclusionary clauses. The realistic approach is preferable to the technical approach.]

The Pennsylvania Mutual Life Insurance Company filed a petition for writ of certiorari in the Supreme Court in the *Beley* case on June 22, 1953, but it does not appear from examination of the briefs that a federal question is clearly, if at all, presented, and it is doubtful if the Supreme Court will take jurisdiction on this application. I call attention to the statement by Mr. Samuel J. Goldstein, attorney for the plaintiff in the *Beley* case, contained in an article entitled "The War Clause in Life Insurance Contracts" (Insurance Law Journal, July, 1953, at page 458) in which he says that no federal or constitutional question was raised during the proceedings and arguments in the *Beley* case and that it would appear to be a foregone conclusion that the writ of certiorari would be denied. If the Supreme Court does deny the petition for writ of certiorari in the *Beley* case, the fact that no federal or constitutional question was presented should be sufficient to rebut any argument that the Supreme Court of the United States, by a denial of the writ, has approved the decision of the Supreme Court of Pennsylvania in the *Beley* case.

• • •

It is believed that the Korean conflict was a war in every sense of the word—actually, legally and constitutionally. It was certainly a war as that term is used in private contracts and for a court to hold otherwise it is necessary for the court to rewrite the contract of insurance and impose a limitation on the exclusion of liability.

25. Anderson, William D. Insurance war clauses–judicial notice –Korea. *Georgia Bar Journal,* v. 16, November 1953, pp. 217-218.

    [Held that the court in *Beley* failed to take into account the many affirmative acts of Congress. The author cites precedent to support judicial notice of the public and private acts of the legislative, executive and judicial branches.]

26. Bennett, William C. Recent Decisions. Insurance–Korean conflict is war within the meaning of the word war in life insurance policies. *Georgetown Law Journal,* v. 42, November 1953, pp. 155-157.

    [The article compares the definition of war in three cases–*Weissman, Bennion* and *Durham*–with definition in *Beley* and *Harding*. This comparison demonstrates that a cleavage is developing in the law on this point.]

In conclusion, while recognizing the practical difficulty set up by the Supreme Court of Pennsylvania, as to the definite standard which should be used to decide whether a "conflict" or an "incident" is a "war" within the meaning of the war clause in an insurance policy, nevertheless, we are forced to agree that the *Weissman* case illustrates the better and wider prevailing law. Since the insured does not sit with a "lawyer at his elbow", it is only realistic to assume that the terms of the contract should be given a real and practical interpretation, rather than a strictly technical one. Otherwise the burden on the insured would be too ponderous. War in the real and practical sense involves the "hazards to human life", which certainly existed in Korea, and the courts should not be required to "affect a technical ignorance of actualities."

27. Short, Reuben. Insurance–military or naval service–war. *University of Kansas Law Review,* v. 2, December 1953, pp. 194-197.

    [Held that no case to date seems to have been so arbitrary in its construction of the word "war" as *Harding*. This case seems to have exceeded the limits of fairness in an effort to protect the insured.]

28. Creveling, Wilbur C. Insurance–termination of war clause —the Korean war. *Temple Law Quarterly,* v. 26, Winter 1953, pp. 336-340.

[Held that the Korean war was authorized by authority of Congress, the war-making power of our government, under provisions of the Mutual Defense Act of 1949. Courts have previously taken judicial notice of undeclared wars, and this war is an actual war by the authority of Congress. The court could have taken judicial notice if it had desired to, which it should have done. The meaning given to a word by parties to a contract should control.]

29. Charles, W. Norman, Jr. Insurance—recovery under double indemnity provision for accidental death denied where insured was killed in a plane crash while in military service "in time of war," since Korean conflict was "war" within meaning of the policy's exemption. *Georgetown Law Journal,* v. 42 (1953-1954), pp. 318-322.
[Held that the reasoning of *Meadows* (at this date the most recent appellate decision) would best serve as the pattern for consideration in any subsequent litigation on this question. It remains to be seen whether courts in future cases will follow *Beley* and *Harding* or *Meadows.*]

30. Cody, Edward C. Life insurance—war exclusion clause—Korean conflict. *St. Louis University Law Journal,* v. 3, Fall 1954, pp. 221-225.
[Discussing *Langlas* and other recent cases, held that the majority view in *Langlas* seems to be better. The real purpose of exclusionary clauses is to protect against abnormal and excessive risk in war, declared or undeclared. The modern type of war modifies the concept of its initiation. Probably there will be changes in policy clauses.]

31. [No author] Life insurance—war clause—Korean conflict. *Vanderbilt Law Review,* v. 7, February 1954, pp. 295-299.
[Held that the realistic interpretation in *Weissman* "appears sound in theory," but many courts may continue a legalistic interpretation which makes the losses of insurance companies imposed ultimately on the public. So it would seem that the realistic approach may well be as sound on policy grounds as it is in theory. The problem suggests the need for a uniform war clause.]

32. Marshall, John G. The war clause in life insurance contracts. *Utah Law Review,* v. 4, Spring 1954, pp. 120-129.

[Held that reason would seem to support the view that the word "war" in an exclusion clause of a life insurance contract should be interpreted in its common rather than technical sense. Recent holdings have created a good deal of confusion, but the legal question concerning the definition of "war" in the Korean cases is "quite simple: Is the word 'war' to be interpreted as it is commonly understood, or in its technical 'legal' sense?" The ambiguity in war clauses is of the making of the insurance companies. More careful drafting would eliminate most ambiguities, and several suggestions are made.]

33. Kleiman, Raymond. Insurance—military exclusion clauses—Korean war—"act of war" interpreted. *Temple Law Quarterly*, v. 31, Fall 1957, pp. 81-85.

[Discussing a recently decided Pennsylvania case, *Thomas,* held that the Supreme Court of that state appears, without specifically saying so, to have overruled its earlier case, *Beley*. In *Thomas* the court construed the term "act of war" as an unambiguous one, used in its common, non-technical sense according to the intention of the parties to the insurance contract.]

In 1953, the Pennsylvania Supreme Court decided the case of *Beley* v. *Pennsylvania Mutual Life Ins. Co.* That case concerned a policy using the phrase "in time of war." The court there ruled that the Korean war was not "war" in its "constitutional" or "legal" sense and that the plaintiff could recover the additional amount. By its decision in the instant case, it appears that the court has overruled the *Beley* case without specifically saying so. It may be that the court by a strained reasoning still desired the *Beley* case to "cling to its bosom." Nevertheless, the proposition in the instant case represents a view that is currently gaining momentum in other jurisdictions. Even though public opinion is sympathetic to the fighting man, the courts should not lose sight of the fact that proper interpretation of any contract is based on the intention of the parties, express and implied, and not on artificial technicalities that may hinder the administration of justice. The Pennsylvania Supreme Court, by this decision, has made a significant contribution to the ever-increasing case law which takes a realistic view of the problems of military exclusion clauses.

34. [No author] Insurance—"act of war" defined. *Fordham Law Review*, v. 26, Autumn 1957, pp. 574-577.

[Discussing *Thomas,* held that the Pennsylvania Supreme Court should have expressly overruled *Beley.* The liberal interpretation of the word "war" is the more reasonable because it gives effect to the obvious intent of the parties concerned. Although this may require the courts to determine what constitutes war, it avoids any fine distinctions and artificial standards which prejudice the meaning of the contract.]

35. Carney, Edward J., Jr. Insurance—double indemnity clause —war exclusion. *Villanova Law Review,* v. 3, no. 1, November 1957, pp. 107-109.

[No specific definition of "war" was submitted by the author. The article includes discussion of *Thomas.* The following quotation contains discussion of the results of that case.]

In considering the phrase "act of war" as a unit, the court found that it was not ambiguous, consistently meaning hostilities between nations, whether in declared or undeclared wars.[9*] Therefore the principle of interpreting the contract against the insurer was not applied in the instant case as it was in the *Beley* case. Considerable authority for the conclusion that undeclared wars are included in war exemption clauses may be found in other jurisdictions.[10*]

The question may be considered open in Pennsylvania since the instant case casts serious doubts on the underlying attitude of the court in the *Beley* case. The instant case shows a willingness on the part of the court to take judicial notice of the Korean conflict as being a "war" in common parlance. In the *Beley* case the court said that the existence or nonexistence of war was a political, not a judicial question.[11*] However the instant case indicates that the court could no longer close its judicial eyes to what everyone else called a war.[12] In so doing they have substituted a

*Footnotes 9-11 omitted.

[12] A strong argument could be made that Congress recognized the fact of war in Korea even though they did not choose to declare it, by its extension of the "G.I. Bill" to Korean veterans, and its appropriations in support of combat operations in that area.

very unpredictable standard for the formal congressional declaration of war in interpreting insurance contracts.[13] It is now left to the court to determine, by a scale known only to itself,[14] whether a particular clash of arms is a war within the meaning of a particular war exclusion clause. This problem need not arise in future policies since insurance contracts can, and should, be drafted so as to cover any clash of arms in a declared or undeclared war but as for the policies already issued, each case must be decided on its own particular facts.

36. Albus, William N. War exclusion clauses. *Life Association News,* v. 67, January 1972, pp. 67-70.

The use of the term "war" has created innumerable issues both as to its duration and even its existence. Recent situations, such as the attack on Pearl Harbor and the Korean Conflict, have been responsible for a flurry of litigation. The question in these instances and others of a similar nature is whether the term "war" should be construed in the legal or technical sense, when there is an official declaration of war by Congress; or in the broadest sense, when it is given its common ordinary meaning. The two concepts may be differentiated as *legal war* and *material war.* On this point the cases are in irreconcilable conflict and the

---

[13]It is suggested that once a court assumes that the term "war" means what the general public considers to be a war the problem arises as to how and where the line will be drawn. Under this interpretation, how would the court decide a truce line incident? When did Korea become a war? Would the deciding factor be when the first United States troops were ordered into the field or after a year of combat, or possibly after the newspapers began to refer to it as a war? This lack of definite standard will make predictability extremely low in this area, to say the least.

[14]Its search for a scale could lead a court to consider the particular circumstances surrounding the formation of an insurance contract in question. The insurer could then offer an argument based on actuarial figures. For example, the insurer manifests a clear intention not to cover military risks by the inclusion of a war exclusion clause in its contract. The insurer then bases the insured's premiums on the ordinary risks of the average person and to extend coverage to a war risk not intended to be covered by the parties on a technicality is to give a protection for which no premium has been paid.

variety of language of the clauses involved is of little consequence.

Although most of the phrases employed in war clauses may have the same or similar intent, the construction placed upon the individual clause is controlling. Perhaps several recent cases may prove illustrative of the principles embodied in the judicial philosophy on this subject.

• • •

[Three cases—*Jackson, Hammond* and *Beley*—have held that the Korean conflict was not a war because there had not been a congressional declaration and because the state of war is a political and not a judicial question. The "more pragmative" view had been taken in "an impressive number of courts"—*Goodrich, Schneiderman* and *Stanbery* are cited.]

What is "War"?

Obviously, the question of what constitutes a "war" is not judicially settled. It has been pointed out in a report of the Committee on Foreign Affairs of the House of Representatives of the U.S. Congress that during the period between 1798 and 1945 there were some 150 or more occasions on which U.S. military forces were engaged in various countries. The proponents of using a "declared war" as controlling maintain that it would be an impossible task for the courts to determine in each instance and without definite guidelines whether a particular action is or is not a "war" within the contemplation of the parties to the insured contract. The use of the phrase "declared or undeclared war" in exclusion clauses might help to clarify the matter. Such a clause was contained in one of the contracts at issue in the *Goodrich* case, supra, but unfortunately, determination of its effect was not necessary for the court to reach its conclusion.

One fact is apparent. War exclusion and military service clauses must be carefully drafted to reflect the actual intentions and understandings of the parties to the insurance contract. Perhaps an explanation of the meaning of the clause made a part of or attached as an amendment to the policy and detailing fully the consequences of the language would help to alleviate some of the confusion surrounding this issue. Clearly, although regrettably, the applicability of war exclusion clauses in insurance contracts is not yet moot.

37. Crain, James M. War exclusion clauses and undeclared wars. *Tennessee Law Review*, v. 39, Winter 1972, pp. 328-339.

I. *Introduction*

There was no evidence that the four men dressed in civilian attire who killed Phillip J. Welts and robbed others in his party at gunpoint thirty miles behind the Union lines were Confederate soldiers. Nor did the facts that his work in repairing railroad bridges was of military significance, that he was working under Army orders, and that he was paid by an Army paymaster, make him a soldier. Therefore, said the New York Commissioner of Appeals, Welts' death was not one of the "casualties or consequences of war or rebellion, or from belligerent forces."[1] as was excluded from coverage by his life insurance policy, and the beneficiary could collect the full value.[2] As one of the earliest reported cases dealing with war exclusions in life insurance policies that case is interesting because no one questioned the existence of a war, despite the absence of a Congressional declaration. Yet that question, so blithely ignored a hundred years ago, has been the central issue in at least thirty-one cases since 1941, and no explicit answer has appeared.

It is universally accepted that war exclusion clauses are valid in life insurance policies. It is also universally accepted that when an ambiguity appears in an insurance policy, that ambiguity will be resolved in favor of the insured and against the insuror.[3] Beyond those considerations, agreement ceases. A war exclusion clause raises two questions, and there is a split of authority on both. The first is: was there a war? The second: does the clause exclude coverage only for the results of a war? This comment examines the first of these questions.[4]

• • •

---

[1]Welts v. Connecticut Mutual Insurance Co., 48 N.Y. 34 (1871).

[2]Id. at 34.

[3]See generally 13 Appleman, Insurance Law and Practice §§ 7423-7428 (1943).

[4]The question of "status" exclusion or "result" exclusion has been the more heavily litigated, thirty-one such cases being collected in the *Third Decennial Digest* alone.

V. *Conclusion: Policy Considerations*

It can be assumed, with little fear of contradiction, that the basic intent of an insuror is to avoid liability in all possible situations, and that the basic intent of an insured is to recover the maximum amount possible in all situations. Neither of these intentions should be given the support of a court of law. While the insured should be given the benefit of the doubt in a given situation, a judicial policy uncompromisingly favoring the insured would seem to run counter to accepted rules of jurisprudence. This is particularly true in the case of a war exclusion. Actuarial tables cannot take the effects of war into consideration. While it is unlikely that many insurance companies would fail if they were forced to assume such a risk, such assumption would cause a rise in premiums. Also, it is highly likely that some companies would fail. Neither of these results is desirable. Courts must maintain their neutrality in these situations. In District Judge Wyzanski's words:

> both [i]nsurer and insured are concerned with bullets, not ballots. . . . Where the fray has become a far-ranging set of battles it is what they would, and therefore an interpreting court should, regard as war. . . . The so-called ambiguity [of the word war] is the creation of lawyers not laymen. No unsophisticated mind would question that there was a war in Korea in 1952 . . . [a]nd what a layman can see, is not to be looked at with a squint unfriendly to insurance companies in their capacity as authors. Policies of insurance, like other contracts, must receive a reasonable interpretation consonant with the apparent object and plain intent of the parties. This is entirely consistent with the rule that ambiguities should be construed most favorably to the assured.[57]

The "technical meaning" rule of Pennsylvania and Colorado seems to be a poor one. In the first place it ignores the only valid purpose behind a war exclusion clause. The passing of a resolution by Congress does not increase the risk to servicemen in the absence of actual military operations, and the risk inherent in such operations is not decreased by the absence of a declaration of war. Since a technical state of war is irrelevant to the risks insured

[57]Gagliormella v. Metropolitan Life Ins. Co., 122 F. Supp. 246, 249 (D. Mass. 1954).

against, it should not be determinative of liability in the absence of a clearly stated intent that it be determinative. Secondly, requiring that words be given a meaning different from that of common usage will inevitably tend to benefit that party which is aware of the special meaning—in this case, the insurer. The insured layman will read something into the policy that is not there, and either fail to claim what is due or believe himself covered when he is not. That result should be avoided.

The most cogent objection to using the word *war* in its ordinary meaning seems to be that neither insurer nor insured will be aware of when the exclusion operates because of the difficulty, in the absence of a declaration, of determining when a state of war exists. That uncertainty, universal under the "common meaning" rule, would be limited to the insured if the technical meaning were used. And the test used in *Schneiderman*[58]—operations intended to gain a military advantage—may remove much of the uncertainty in the determination of when a state of war exists. For example, it makes clear the difference between the attack on the *Panay* in 1937 and the attack on Pearl Harbor. It does not answer all questions, but no test can be expected to do that. It does provide a reasonably objective standard with which to judge borderline cases.

The "inherently ambiguous" rule is superior to the "technical meaning" rule in that any uncertainty that arises could not possibly work against a layman in court. The possibility remains that a layman might fail to make a claim in the belief that the exclusion clause applies. Also, this theory ignores the purpose of the war exclusion to the same extent as the Pennsylvania rule. Judge Wyzanski's remark that the ambiguity is the creation of lawyers[59] is not necessarily either pertinent or correct; most people are aware of the constitutional provisions regarding declarations of war. Yet there is one further objection which applies equally to both the "technical meaning" and the "inherently ambiguous" rules.

Justice Musmanno, in his concurring opinion in the *Beley* decision, speculated that there might well be no more

---

[58]Schneiderman v. Metropolitan Casualty Company of New York, 14 App. Div. 2d 284, 286, 220 N.Y.S. 2d 947, 949 (1961).

[59]122 F. Supp. at 249.

declarations of war by the United States.[60] The history of the world since the end of World War II makes that speculation prophetic. This author is not aware of a single conflict in the past twenty-six years which was formalized by a declaration of war. Yet that period has been as bloody and conflict-ridden as any in the history of the world. The future shows no signs of being either more peaceful or more formal. If this is to be the pattern for the remainder of this century, the adoption of either the "technical meaning" rule or the "inherently ambiguous" rule will tend to make the simple war exclusion clause a legal nullity. To be effective under these theories, a clause might need to be so detailed and involved that few laymen could understand its provisions. So long as laymen purchase insurance in the absence of legal advice—and the practice can be expected to continue indefinitely—the courts should avoid technical constructions of the policies they buy.

[60] 373 Pa. at 239, 95 A.2d at 221.

5

PROPOSED REFORMS

The opinions of members of the courts in the many cases involving definition of "war" in life insurance contracts, and the articles on the subject published in professional journals, have dealt almost entirely with the judicial definition of the term. Few suggestions have been made for changes to be effected by the insurance companies, and even fewer suggestions were made for legislative action. Three general classes of such suggestions are: (1) adoption of a uniform war clause which will be given uniform construction; (2) statutory changes in wording, including a few proposals that the government should bear the risk; and (3) assumption of responsibility by the insurance companies for more careful drafting of their policies, including recommendations for specific, unambiguous wording.

Several articles in professional journals dealt with the broader subject of the proper form and content of life insurance policies.

The following portions of this section contain excerpts from articles in professional journals and from opinions of the court, in the 1947-1975 period.

Particular attention is called to:

Krohn, W. O. Insurance—extent of loss and liability of insurer—whether or not fact death occurred in military service precludes recovery on life insurance policy containing military service clause. *Chicago–Kent Law Review,* v. 25, March 1947, pp. 171-176.

Brown, Wendell J. War clause of the next war. *Insurance Law Journal,* v. 1948, May 1948, pp. 382-394.

Billings, Robert B. Of war clauses. *Insurance Law Journal,* v. 1952, December 1952, pp. 793-806.

Albus, William N. War exclusion clauses. *Life Association News*, v. 67, January 1972, pp. 67-70.

Crain, James M. War exclusion clauses and undeclared wars. *Tennessee Law Review*, v. 37, Winter 1972, pp. 328-333.

1. Krohn, W. O. Insurance—extent of loss and liability of insurer—whether or not fact death occurred in military service precludes recovery on life insurance policy containing military service clause. *Chicago-Kent Law Review*, v. 25, March 1947, pp. 171-176, at pp. 175-176.

   > Definition and comparison, then, do not resolve the problem, for there are no well-defined "rules." Objective analysis demonstrates that the genesis of the problem lies in the need for judicial construction of "ambiguous" exemption clauses. The obvious remedial action is to reexamine the verbiage used in the policy, for a concise, clear, complete exemption should leave no room for ambiguity and consequent construction. Certainty of exemption would not only benefit both insured and insurer but would minimize the need for judicial construction.[39]

2. (No author) Date of war inception as determinant of liability in life insurance contracts. *Yale Law Journal*, v. 56, April 1947, pp. 746-752, at p. 752.

   > Insurance company draftsmanship would still not bear too onerous a burden in excepting the risk of death resulting from armed conflict lacking a formal war label; other insurers have been more explicit on this same issue.[49*] Nor would it have involved the foresight of a seer; the history of our relations with other nations has not been devoid of such incidents.[50*]

3. Opinion of the U.S. Court of Appeals of the District of Columbia, *Stinson v. New York Life Insurance Co.*, 67 F. Supp. 860 (1947); 167 F. 2d 233 (1948), at p. 240.

   > We appreciate the fact that insurers face no small problem in framing exclusion clauses, but their draftsman-

---

[39]Changing methods of warfare, new means of starting or "declining" war, as well as increased civilian participation in war activities pose additional problems for the framers of exemption clauses.

*Footnotes 49-50 omitted.

ship does not bear too onerous a burden to make more explicit, to the minds of laymen, the extent of the meaning of such a phrase as "engaged in war." We need not emphasize the ease with which ambiguity inherent in that phrase, in this manner of usage, could have been avoided.

4. Brown, Wendell J. War clause of the next war. *Insurance Law Journal,* v. 1948, May 1948, pp. 382-394, at p. 390.

 Accordingly if an insurer decides that it is not able actuarially to cover a potential risk of deaths outside the home areas after an unconditional surrender and before the formal declaration of the termination of war, it will have to do so in specific terminology which cannot be interpreted to apply to merely the cessation of the organized shooting. This could be done in the manner of much of the enabling war legislation. The war clause could provide that such a clause would be operative "during the period of any war, declared or undeclared, and until terminated by Presidential Proclamation or joint resolution of the Congress or by treaty of peace, whichever shall first occur, and not otherwise."

5. Drury, Arthur P. Ambiguity in war clauses. *Insurance Law Journal,* v. 1948, September 1948, pp. 738-743, at p. 742.

 While it is highly desirable that war clauses should be unambiguous, whether or not such a result can ever be attained is subject to some question. Indicative of the inherent difficulty is the construction which has been given to the single word "war" in the war clause, the expression usually being "at war," "in time of war," or "engaged in war."

6. Kastner, Ralph H. War clauses—past and present. *Nebraska Law Review,* v. 30, January 1951, pp. 267-278, at pp. 267-268, 275-276.

 We are again faced with all the strains on our economy that flow from a "war emergency" and, conceivably, that situation may become commonplace for the rest of your natural life and mine. As Cowper so succinctly opined in his "Expostulation" 150 years ago, "War lays a burden on the reeling state."

 In such circumstances, and to a distinguished and educated group like this, it is quite unnecessary for me to recite at length the obvious reasons for a life insurance company to use, necessarily, some form of war clause in the issuance of new policies.

The hazard is one that is not insurable in the ordinary sense. Hence a clause, be it one of limitation or outright exclusion, is an appropriate instrument for the insurer's selection of risks, and serves as a medium to effect equity between all classes of policyholders.

• • •

As is to be expected, difficulty has been encountered in meeting the interpretations by some Commissioners [the Commissioners' Life Committee] of the assumed technicalities of their own state laws, so that it will be difficult, if not impossible, for a company to have one uniform clause which it can use in all jurisdictions if business is done on a Nationwide scale. By the same token, differences of a minor or major character will exist as between clauses used by the several life insurance companies. This should not be too surprising when we note that a study in 1942 of war clauses employed by 174 companies, having more than 93% of the aggregate ordinary insurance in force in the United States at the time, showed that there were no two identical clauses in use. Of equal significance, also, now that insurance has been decreed to be commerce, is the fact that uniformity of company action might give rise to anti-trust implications, fantastic as that observation may appear to the average lawyer.

As recognized by the Joint War Clause Committee of the American Life Convention and Life Insurance Association of America, another facet of the potential war problem, to which experience furnishes no guide, is the probable extent of civilian casualties in the Home Areas in the course of a war fought with modern weapons. Hitherto war restrictions have been limited to deaths while in Service.

It is believed by our Joint Committee that conditions have so changed now that the companies should be permitted to protect themselves through the inclusion in their policies of war restrictions applying both to civilians and those in military service, wherever located. To that end, statutory changes will be necessary in numerous instances and efforts will be made to secure permissive authority when the opportunity affords or the occasion demands.

7. Smith, Calvin E. The meaning and effect of military service and war exclusion clauses in life insurance policies. *Duke Bar Journal*, v. 3, Fall 1952, pp. 11-20, at p. 20.

Conclusion

Military service and war exception clauses are not against public policy. It is a widely recognized right of an insurance company to choose and to limit the kinds of risks it is willing to assume. As has been shown, the advent of the legalistic interpretation of establishing the time when a "war clause" can become operative has worked both for and against the insurer.

Today we are engaged in a United Nations policy action which has the length, breadth and scope of a full scale war. If the few jurisdictions which have taken the legalistic view of "war clauses" stand by this approach and multiply their numbers to a considerable extent, when more and more cases of this nature find their way into their courts, it is inevitable that insurance companies are going to suffer and be forced to alter their policy provisions. Insurance companies can and will revise their acturial tables to include the added risks which may be forced on them in greater numbers than heretofore anticipated.

It is submitted that the problems involved in this particular phase of the law may well result in: (1) new provisions in life insurance policies; (2) legislation defining war and regulating these new provisions; (3) legislation designed to avert a severe strain on insurance companies; and (4) an increasing number of jurisdictions recognizing the Korean hostilities as an actual "war." Again it is emphasized that, since ambiguous terms in an insurance policy are generally construed in favor of the insured and since juries tend to find against the insurer, it is of extreme importance that insurance companies clearly express their intention in the wording of military service and war exception clauses in the policies they issue.

8. Billings, Robert B. Of war clauses. *Insurance Law Journal*, v. 1952, December 1952, pp. 793-806, at pp. 793-794, 806.

Between the outbreak of the American Revolution on

April 19, 1775, and the commencement of World War II on December 7, 1941, the United States was involved in 99 wars, expeditions, campaigns, occupations and other disturbances requiring the use of the army.[1*] That means one such conflict every two years! Number 100, of course, is already in progress, a fact which has caused insurance companies, commissioners, attorneys and policyholders to reconsider and study the efficiacy of war clauses. Military commanders have also been concerned as additional "regulators" by virtue of their power over egress and ingress on military bases. At least one commander has specified that no company can operate on his base unless the policy is free of the war clause.[2*] One novel twist has been proposed to the usual suggestion to permit the government to bear the risk, namely, that the companies write a policy free of the war-risk clause with the understanding that the government will underwrite or reinsure the war-risk.[3] These current difficulties emphasize a basic perennial problem.

The earliest life insurance contracts did not afford protection against the hazards inherent in war. However, the tremendous impact of the Civil War, which commenced on April 15, 1861, led to considerable agitation for life insurance protection for soldiers. On April 25, 1863, the State of New York authorized the National Union Life and Limb Assurance Company to "make insurance on the lives and limbs and health of the officers, soldiers, sailors and marines of the Army and Navy of the United States."[4*] Thus commenced an effort to eliminate the war-risk exclusion from life insurance policies. Today, in time of peace, companies make basic policies war-risk free, although the limitation is retained in supplementary contracts, such as double indemnity or accidental death and disability.

The meaning of the term "war clause" is well known. A war clause is a provision in an insurance policy or rider thereto which relieves the insurance com-

*Footnotes 1, 2, 4 omitted.

[3]The American Life Convention and the Life Insurance Association of America are reported to be studying the proposal, although the origin of the suggestion is unknown. (*The National Underwriter*, March 7, 1952, p. 1).

pany of the full liability for the face value if the loss is caused by war. It is usual to provide for the payment of a reduced amount—such as the amount of the premiums paid, the cash value or the reserve of the policy, or a similar small sum—if death occurs from war.[5*] A war clause is an extraordinary limitation on the contract and requires the written consent of the insured.[6*]

• • •

The war clause in life insurance policies is of immediate and continuing concern to companies, state insurance officials, agents, lawyers and others who are employed in the life insurance industry. Careful consideration of the clause, as has been indicated, provokes deep thought cutting across broad fields of legal and actuarial knowledge. It is of vital concern to policyholders and the general public. The war clause does not represent a cynical attitude toward patriotism but a pragmatic effort to fuse the interests of companies, policyholders and prospective policyholders. Careful study of the war clause will continue as long as there are wars, and it is my hope that this article will be helpful in that further consideration of this perennial problem.

9. Serino, Rosemarie. Insurance-Constitutional law—two recent cases, *Harding v. Pennsylvania Mutual Life Ins. Co.*, 171 Pa. 236, 90 A.2d 589 (1952) and *Beley v. Pennsylvania Mutual Life Ins. Co.*, 171 Pa. 253, 90 A.2d 597 (1952). *Catholic University of America Law Review*, v. 3, January 1953, pp. 60-62, at p. 62.

   It is clear that the insurance companies are faced with a difficult task in framing war exclusion clauses due to the ambiguity inherent in word usage. The remedy for this apparent difficulty would be a uniform war clause for life insurance policies in which the word "war" is unambiguously defined, thereby eliminating the necessity of judicial interpretation.

10. Wheeler, J. W. The war clause. *Insurance Law Journal*, v. 370, November 1953, pp. 727-737, at p. 727.

   It is difficult to see how the all-inclusive word "war," as used in insurance contracts, could be enlarged by

*Footnotes 5, 6 omitted.

adding the words "declared or undeclared," or by the use of any other adjectives. If an undeclared war is not war, nothing is gained by adding the word "undeclared."

11. Bennett, William C. Recent decisions. Insurance–Korean conflict is a war within the meaning of the word war in life insurance policies. *Georgetown Law Journal,* v. 42, November 1953, pp. 155-157, at p. 157.

    The court [in the *Weissman* Case] indicated that the only standard would be the political declaration, or lack of such declaration, by the Congress. Therefore if the insurance companies meant to include undeclared war as well as declared war in their life insurance policies they should actually indicate this intent.

    It can thus be seen that a cleavage is developing in the law on this point. Many insurance companies have provided against such decisions as were given in the Pennsylvania cases, by providing that "war includes undeclared war", or by excluding from the double indemnity provisions any death resulting "wholly or partly from war", or death resulting from war or any "act incident thereto". . . . This action by the insurance companies however, does not settle the legal problem involved.

12. Short, Reuben. Insurance–military or naval service–war. *University of Kansas Law Review,* v. 2, December 1953, p. 194-197, at p. 197.

    For the purpose of protection it would appear from the cases that the language of the termination clauses must be sufficiently all-inclusive to prevent any arbitrary finding of ambiguity by the courts. It is submitted that a phrase such as: "Provision terminates if insured shall at any time engage or enter into military, air or naval service in time of any incident of war, declared or undeclared" would preclude the question and afford complete protection to the insurer.

13. Opinion of the Superior Court of Pennsylvania, *Harding v. Pennsylvania Mut. Life Ins. Co.,* 90 A.2d 589; 171 Pa. Super. 236 (1953), at p. 597.

    Since "war" is a word which has been held to import various meanings, it is incumbent upon the insurer to make clear that it applies to undeclared war, as well as to declared war . . . In our opinion, the insurer has failed to meet the burden cast upon it. The attempt of the appellee to evade liability of double indemnity should not receive judicial condonation. The phraseology of the policy was chosen by the insurer and tendered in fixed form to the prospective policyholder, and since its language is reasonably open to two constructions, we will adopt that construction which is more favorable to the insured.

14. Charles, W. Norman, Jr. Insurance-recovery under double indemnity provision for accidental death denied where insured was killed in a plane crash while in military service "in time of war," since Korean conflict was "war" within meaning of the policy's exemption. *Georgetown Law Journal,* v. 42, November 1953, pp. 318-322, at p. 322.

    Since ambiguous terms in policies are generally construed in favor of the insured (and courts have not been averse to expand the language in finding ambiguities) insurance companies must be emphatic in stating their intentions. Again, the possibility of atomic warfare must now be considered a reality. A potential war problem will be the probable extent of civilian casualties in the home areas in the course of a modern war. Hitherto, the application of war exclusion clauses has been limited to deaths while in military service. Legislation designed to avert severe strains on insurance companies should allow inclusion of war clauses in policies applying to both civilians and those in military service alike.

15. [No author] Life insurance—war clause—Korean conflict. *Vanderbilt Law Review,* v. 7, February 1954, pp. 295-299, at p. 299.

    The whole problem, of course, suggests the need for a uniform war clause which will be given uniform construction.

16. Marshall, John G. The war clause in life insurance contracts. *Utah Law Review,* v. 4, Spring 1954, pp. 120-129, at p. 128.

    Conclusion
    In spite of the variety of the clauses which courts are called upon to apply to diverse situations, the decisions

indicate that the law on exclusion clauses is relatively well settled. Significant inconsistencies and uncertainties are found in only two areas: (1) Whether the word "war" should be understood in its technical or ordinary sense; (2) Whether the words "engaged" and "enrolled" require that a causal connection be shown between death and the military service. In both of these areas the courts show an inclination to resolve the ambiguity in favor of the insured. The insurance companies have no just cause for complaint, however, inasmuch as the ambiguity is of their own making. More careful drafting would eliminate most of the difficulty. As to the first of these areas of uncertainty, if the insurer intends to use "war" in its technical sense it could use some such phrase as "declared war" or, even more explicitly, "Congressionally declared war." The common sense of "war" could perhaps best be indicated by other words—e.g., "actual warfare," "armed hostilities typical of warfare," etc.

17. Cody, Edward C. Life insurance—war exclusion clause—Korean conflict. *St. Louis University Law Journal,* v. 3, Fall 1954, pp. 221-225, at p. 225.

    To avoid the strict rule of resolving ambiguities in favor of the insured,[21*] many insurance companies have revised their war exclusion clauses so as to define the policy coverage in more explicit terms of modern warfare and international relations.[22*] Perhaps the use of the expression "declared or undeclared war" will . . . accomplish this feat.

18. Dissenting Opinion of Justice Musmanno, of the Supreme Court of Pennsylvania, in the case of *Francis R. Thomas, Sr., Appellant, v. Metropolitan Life Insurance Company;* 131 A.2d 600 (1957); 388 Pa. 499 (1957), at pp. 611-612, 618-619.

    There is no doubt that Francis Thomas was killed in battle. Was that battle-death the kind of death which was excluded from the insurance policy of which the plaintiff in this case is the beneficiary? The answer to that question is not to be found alone amid the smoke and acrid smell of gunpowder on the bleak, cold

* **Footnotes 21, 22 omitted.**

Korean Hill which witnessed the heroic and glorious death of Francis Thomas. It is to be found also in the carpeted, comfortable, and commodious offices of the Metropolitan Life Insurance Company where its skilled, expert, and experienced lawyers drafted the contract which was to become the insurance policy purchased by 17-year-old Francis Thomas. What did these lawyers have in mind when they said that their company would not pay double indemnity in the event that insured came to his death as the result of an act of war? What language did they employ in expressing the contingency under which the company would not be required to pay the additional sum stipulated in the policy? They knew that under Article I, Section 8, Clause 11, of the United States Constitution, only Congress can declare war and that, therefore, a state of war can come into being only when the elected representatives of the people of the United States by suitable legislation so pronounce. Thus, in preparing the formal instrument which was to bind their master, the lawyers would naturally adopt formal language, and we can only conclude that when they used the word "war" they could only mean war in its constitutional sense. . . . only Congress can declare war. The Metropolitan Life Insurance Company's legal staff knew that when they expressed a certain contingency through the medium of the word "war", only a certain legal status could result from the use of that word, and the Metropolitan Life Insurance Company must be held accountable for the employment of that word in its formal and documentary sense. If the Metropolitan legal staff had wanted to exclude conflicts which were not constitutionally declared wars, they could have done this clearly, neatly, and easily. All they had to do was to add after the word, "war", the words "declared or undeclared." But they did not do this and we have no authority to excuse that omission by speculation or rationalization, or, least of all, on some arbitrary theory which saves the company from a voluntarily assumed contracted obligation.

What is war and what is not war has been decided by the Courts of the Nation so often that no lawyer, or insurance policy drafter, can plead ignorance on the subject.

• • •

To allow the defendant insurance company in the case at bar to escape liability is to put a premium on contractual looseness. In the *Beley* case, Chief Justice Stern said (273 Pa. 231, 95A.2d 205):

"A policy of life insurance is a highly technical instrument, drawn up presumably with meticulous care by legal experts on behalf of the Insurance Company, and who not only intend to use all terms in their legal sense but know how to accomplish that result; it may be assumed, therefore, that if defendant had here meant to invest the term 'war' with a broader connotation than its 'constitutional' or 'legal' intendment, it would have effected this by the addition of words indicating such an intention, as, for example, 'declared or undeclared' war."

We thus ruled that if an insurance company prefers to use language which makes it liable under certain conditions, when it could by a slight modification exonerate itself from such liability, it uses such language at its peril. Why does not that rule apply in the present Thomas case?

• • •

Of all contracts, the insurance policy should be the most clearly worded. When a person purchases a policy with benefits payable to those he loves, he wants to give to those endeared ones not a sword with which to fight a bitter and costly legal battle, but a vehicle in which they may ride over the lonely and rocky road he leaves behind him.

• • •

Why should the right of a beneficiary under an insurance policy have to depend upon commas, semicolons and exhausting reasoning that might be applicable to an algebraic problem but hardly consonant with the simple duty of doing justice under a contract whose intent and purpose are clear?

19. Carney, Edward J., Jr. Insurance-double indemnity clause—war exclusion. *Villanova Law Review,* v. 3, November 1957, pp. 107-109, at p. 109.

This problem need not arise in future policies since insurance contracts can, and should, be drafted so as to cover any clash of arms in a declared or undeclared war but as for the policies already issued, each case must be decided on its own particular facts.

20. Opinion of the New York Supreme Court, Appellate Division, First Department in the case of *Schneiderman v. Metropolitan Cas. Co. of N.Y.*, 220 N.Y.S. 2d 947 (1961): 86 A.L.C. 119 (1961): at pp. 950, 952.

    We are to take cognizance of the fact that an insurance policy is generally a contract with the average man who presumably is unfamiliar with the existence of a state of war from the strictly political, military and/or legal standpoint. Such a man would read the term war in a policy exclusory clause in the sense that the term is commonly used and understood in the every day expression rather than as used and understood in international relations or military affairs.

    • • •

    The uncertainty in the language used is chargeable to the company, and any doubt in the construction to be adopted must be resolved against it.

21. Albus, William N. War exclusion clauses. *Life Association News,* v. 67, January 1972, pp. 67-70, at p. 70.

    The proponents of using a "declared war" as controlling maintain that it would be an impossible task for the courts to determine in each instance and without definite guidelines whether a particular action is or is not a "war" within the contemplation of the parties to the insured contract. The use of the phrase "declared or undeclared war" in exclusion clauses might help to clarify the matter. Such a clause was contained in one of the contracts at issue in the *Goodrich* case, supra, but unfortunately, determination of its effect was not necessary for the court to reach its conclusion.

    One fact is apparent. War exclusion and military service clauses must be carefully drafted to reflect the actual intentions and understanding of the parties to the insurance contract. Perhaps an explanation of the meaning of the clause made a part of or attached as an amendment to the policy and detailing fully the consequences of the language would help to alleviate some of the confusion surrounding this issue. Clearly, although regrettably, the applicability of war exclusion clauses in insurance contracts is not yet moot.

TABLE OF CASES

(in chronological order, as they appear in the text)

1. West v. Palmetto State Life Ins. Co. 25 S.E. 2d 475 (1943), 202 S.C. 422 (1943).
2. Rosenau v. Idaho Mut. Ben. Ass'n. 145 P. 2d 227 (1944); 65 Idaho 408 (1944).
3. Savage v. Sun Life Assur. Co. of Canada. 57 F. Supp. 620 (1944).
4. Gladys Ching Pang v. Sun Life Assurance Company of Canada. 37 Hawaiian Reports 208 (1945).
5. Stankus v. New York Life Insurance Co. 44 N.E. 2d 687 (1942); 312 Mass. 366 (1942).
6. New York Life Ins. Co. v. Bennion. 158 F. 2d 260 (1946); 331 U.S. 811 (1946); 331 U.S. 867 (1946).
7. Stinson v. New York Life Insurance Co. 69 F. Supp. 860 (1947); 167 F. 2d 233 (1948).
8. New York Life Ins. Co. v. Durham. 166 F. 2d 874 (1948).
9. Trimble v. Western and Southern Life Ins. Co. 82 N.E. 2d 548 (1948).
10. National Life and Accident Ins. Co. Inc. v. Leverett. 215 S.W. 2d 939 (1948).
11. Mutual Life Ins. Co. of N.Y. v. Davis. 53 S.E. 2d 571 (1949); 79 Ga. App. 336 (1949).
12. Darnall v. Day. 37 N.W. 2d 277 (1949); 240 Iowa 665 (1949).
13. Beley v. Pennsylvania Mut. Life Ins. Co. 90 A. 2d 597 (1952); 171 Pa. Super. Ct. 253 (1953); 95 A. 2d 202 (1953); 373 Pa. 231 (1953); 346 U.S. 820 (1953).

14. Harding v. Pennsylvania Mut. Life Ins. Co. 90 A. 2d 589 (1952); 171 Pa. Super. 236 (1953); 95 A. 2d. 221 (1953); 373 Pa. 270 (1953); 346 U.S. 812 (1953).
15. Hawkins v. Metrop. Mutual Assurance Co. 69 Am. Life Conv. Legal Bull. 52 (1953).
16. Gray v. Southern Aid Life Ins. Co. 15 C.C.H. Life Cases 507 (1952).
17. Weissman v. Metropolitan Life Ins. Co. 112 F. Supp. 420 (1953).
18. Stanbery v. Aetna Life Ins. Co. 98 A. 2d 134 (1953); 26 N.J. Super. 498 (1953).
19. Western Reserve Life Ins. Co. v. Meadows. 256 S.W. 2d 674 (1953); 261 S.W. 2d 554 (1953); 152 Tex. Sup. Ct. Rep. 559 (1953); 347 U.S. 928 (1954).
20. Podos et al. v. Equitable Life Assur. Society of U.S. 1 C.C.H. Life Cases 2d 757 (1953-1955).
21. Langlas v. Iowa Life Ins. Co. 63 N.W. 2d 885 (1954); 245 Iowa 713 (1954).
22. Gagliormella v. Metropolitan Life Ins. Co. 122 F. Supp. 246 (1954).
23. Carius v. New York Life Ins. Co. 124 F. Supp. 388 (1954).
24. Helen Gudewicz v. John Hancock Mutual Life Insurance Company. 122 N.E. 2d 900 (1954); 331 Mass. 752 (1954).
25. Robert J. Lynch v. The National Life and Accident Insurance Company. 278 S.W. 2d 32 (1955).
26. Martin Christensen v. Sterling Insurance Company. 284 P. 2d 287 (1955); 46 Wash. 2d 713 (1955).
27. Samuel N. Wilkinson and Mary A. Wilkinson v. The Equitable Life Assurance Society of the United States. 151 N.Y.S. 1018 (1956); 2 Misc. 2d 249 (1956).
28. Pyramid Life Insurance Company v. John William Masch. 299 P. 2d 117 (1956); 134 Colo. 70 (1956).
29. Anna Zaccardo v. John Hancock Mutual Life Insurance Co. 124 A. 2d 926 (1956); 20 Conn. Sup. 76 (1956).
30. Francis R. Thomas, Sr. v. Metropolitan Life Insurance Company. 131 A. 2d 600 (1957); 388 Pa. 499 (1957).
31. Constance Zaytoun Lamar v. John Hancock Mutual Life

Insurance Company. 107 S.E. 2d 65 (1959); 249 N.C. 643 (1959).

32. Schneiderman v. Metropolitan Cas. Co. of N.Y. 220 N.Y.S. 2d 947 (1961); 86 A.L.C. 119 (1961).
33. Goodrich v. John Hancock Mut. Life Ins. Co. of Boston. 234 N.Y.S. 2d 587 (1962); 17 App. Div. 2d 271 (1962).
34. Marian Ford Stucker v. The College Life Insurance Company of America. 208 N.E. 2d 731 (1965); 139 Ind. App. 422 (1965).
35. Hammond v. National Life & Accident Ins. Co. 243 S. 2d 902 (1971); 1971 Life Cases (unbound) 329 (1971).
36. Jackson v. N. America Assurance Society of Virginia, Inc. 183 S.E. 2d 160 (1971); 212 Va. 177 (1971).

INDEX

Several portions of this study constitute special indexes. See the following portions of the study:

(1) Table of Contents

The subheadings under the titles of the first three chapters indicate those portions of the text which deal with definitions of war found in judicial decisions in the period 1945-1975. These subheadings indicate decisions in which armed conflicts occurring during that period were held to be "war" and those in which these conflicts were held not to be "war."

(2) Introduction (pp. 1-3)

The purposes of the study and description of its contents amplify the analysis in the Table of Contents.

(3) Articles in Professional Journals (pp. 120-121)

A. Chronological Outline of Articles

This outline indicates articles quoted in Section B in which the authors supported the position that the armed conflicts under discussion were "wars," or the position that they were not.

(4) Table of Cases (pp. 156-158)

The cases analyzed in the study appear in the text in the chronological order in which they are listed in this Table.

